ITALIAN PHRASEBOOK FOR ADULT BEGINNERS: SPEAK ITALIAN IN 30 DAYS!

Common Italian Words & Phrases For Everyday Conversation and Travel

Table of Contents

CLAIM YOUR BONUSES

Italian Video Course Masterclass

Italian Flash Pack

Italian Audio Pronunciations

Italian Travel Guide

Italian Stories Audiobook

Italian Conversations Narrated

Scan QR code to claim your bonuses

— OR —

visit bit.ly/4fyisLd

Introduction

"To have another language is to possess a second soul."
- Charlemagne

1. Aim of the book

Italian is a rather difficult language: grammar, conjugations, pronunciation... there are plenty of head-scratchers. But the worst part is that Italian is even more beautiful than it is difficult. It's a neat, precise, sweet language that just won't let you off the hook; once you fall in love with Italian – you're doomed.

An increasing number of people choose to learn Italian: travelers, musicians, food lovers, fashion enthusiasts, people with Italian ancestry, and many more. This language is mostly learned out of passion, rather than necessity.

So, what's the best way to follow your heart and get to learn Italian? There are different methods to learn a language. The most classic ways involve grammar books, a dictionary, and lots and lots of practice. But that is not for everybody.

The aim of this book is to provide <u>a useful and simple tool to start learning Italian off the right food, but in an easy, fun, and low-pressure way</u>. The scope of this book is not linear academic learning, but a more simple and quicker way to get started with Italian in a more dynamic way.

Alongside learning, this book will provide a <u>collection of useful phrases and vocabulary for travelers and tourists</u>, which will have in this guide a handy instrument to experience Italy to the fullest.

2. Our learning

This book intends to help learning Italian through a <u>motivational-based approach</u>.

The number one reason for giving up on learning a language is loss of motivation; all kinds of learning come with some amount of struggle, and only the desire to move forward will push you through it.

This book will not try to teach Italian in a typical way, with a major focus on grammar and pronunciation, but will help you learn through mistakes, which is the fastest and most natural way to learn.

Along with the more appealing method, we will set daily goals to keep you motivated and for you to challenge yourself and <u>learn the basics of Italian in only 30 days</u>!

Our program is divided into 22 "lessons" that are grouped in 4 parts; each part has a practice section at the end. The idea is for you to take up a lesson a day, with a day for practice at the end of each part, and finish your learning in 26 days. For the last four days, there's a dedicated section to practice with all you have learned throughout the book, with all-encompassing exercises.

Now, without further ado, let's get learning! First, we'll look into the intricacies of learning Italian as an English speaker and into the role of the language barrier while visiting Italy. This is meant to give you a general understanding of what you will be going through and set you up for the lessons.

3. The language barrier

Visiting a foreign country, or simply having to do with someone who comes from a different culture than ours, is a beautiful mind-opening experience, but it can sometimes be a bit of a challenge.

It can be difficult or feel unnatural to communicate with someone who speaks a different language, because we can't do the same things we normally would with people who speak our same language. It's a unique experience that will make your brain function differently in order to face the unusual situation. This is one of the reasons why learning a language helps improve brain functions and keeps our mind young and efficient in the long run. Also, this different functioning of the brain makes you experience life differently, to the point where you develop a sort of second personality or, to get back to our initial quote from Charlemagne, a second soul.

These are the reasons why many people believe that the personal growth you achieve is worth the challenge and the struggle. With this being said, let's now focus on Italian and the specifics of that language barrier.

Most typically, Italians (or Italian speakers) who travel to English-speaking countries tend to have a sufficient knowledge of the English language. So, in that scenario, the language barrier should be relatively thin, and cooperation should bring about a nice mutual understanding.

When traveling to Italy, the situation might be a little different, as you can't expect everybody there to speak fluent English. But don't think it's all the other way around, with no Italians knowing any English. As a matter of fact, many Italians do speak some English, because of a few reasons. Globalization and mass media are the first obvious reasons, as it is hard to live in the 21st century without any knowledge of English, especially if you spend a lot of time online. The second reason is that, in Italy, studying English in school is mandatory by law, since 1962 (initially French was also an option).

For these reasons, most Italians with a decent education that are younger than sixty years old are likely to speak at least basic English. Younger people, let's say forty or younger, usually have a more advanced knowledge of English, because of the internet and social media.

So, when you are in Italy, it will be possible for you to use English or support yourself with it. Most of the people who work at places like stations, airports, hotels, museums, and such have a very high level of English. Police forces in Italy also require a minimum level of English for their officers, although their actual language skills are often not exceptional. If you need to call 911 (which is 112 in Italy), you can safely speak English to the operator.

Around cities, Milan being the best example, most people speak good English, and you'll most likely be able to ask for directions, buy at the local shops, and go to restaurants and pubs with no big issues.

The story might be different when your scenario takes place in the countryside, with a situation that, on average, is a little worse in the south of the country. In fact, as you step away from the cities, it is more likely to find people who are a little less educated and, on average, older.

All considered, it is most useful to know some Italian if you are planning to leave the cities, enjoy nature, and shop from local farmers. In other words, if you want to experience the old rural Italy outside tourist destinations.

Let's now close this part of the topic and start talking about the intricacies of the two languages per se. Italian and English are pretty different languages, but there's a solid common base. The whole of the Italian language and a good half of the English language both come from Latin, which means that around 50%

of English words have an Italian cognate with the exact same root word. Easy examples of this can be terrore (terror), indulgente (indulgent), fatto (fact), and many more.

So, even though the pronunciation and cadence are different, a good portion of the vocabulary is not that far apart. Unfortunately, we also have to consider that there are a number of false friends (similar words with a different meaning), which we will discuss in a dedicated section of the book. Examples of this can be argomento (topic), estate (summer), rumore (noise), etc.

All considered, the main difficulties in learning Italian for an English speaker are three: pronunciation, grammar, and wording.

Italian pronunciation is not particularly difficult, especially in comparison with other languages, but it does have some peculiarities that English speakers find hard to replicate. The most classic examples include double consonants and the letters R, C, and G.

Italian grammar is quite complicated, because Italian comes from Latin and Latin was a very precise and specific language. Italian declensions got fortunately lost, so nouns do not change in relation with their role in the sentence (e.g., if it is the subject or a direct object or other), but verb conjugation is much more detailed than in English.

Last but not least, the sentence construction and wording can be quite different, especially with verbs such as piacere (to like), sentire (to feel) and a few other specific situations.

All considered, there's nothing too difficult you have to worry about. Feel free to make mistakes, because that's what learners do after all, and don't aim for perfection, aim for whatever spikes your motivation, so that you'll build up consistent and productive learning. And have fun! Because having fun can be extremely productive.

PART ZERO

PRONUNCIATION AND GRAMMAR PILLS

0.1
Italian pronunciation
for beginners

In this first chapter, our main focus will be pronunciation. The goal is to give you all the basic instruments to start reading Italian in your head with the correct pronunciation. As you keep on reading, you're going to be exposed to a lot of new Italian words, and it's best if you learn them with the correct pronunciation from the very beginning.

Considering that this is a book for beginners, our focus will be the pronunciation of letters and some tricky clusters of letters.

Although you can reach an acceptable pronunciation by learning from this book alone, books are understandably not the best instrument to study pronunciation, as reading is a very indirect way to learn sounds. For more efficient learning, the best way to go is to use the audiobook version of this book as well. If you feel the need to diversify the material you're exposed to, you can dig into video material you can find online or on Netflix, for example, with movies and shows being the best option.

One thing you have to understand about Italy is that regional accents can vary significantly. If you learn the accent from a YouTuber or influencer, you might learn a regional accent and, consequently, struggle to understand other accents. On the contrary, if you learn spoken Italian from movies and TV shows, you will most likely be exposed to a standard Italian accent, which will make it easier for you to understand other accents.

Language-exchange communities are also a great place to practice pronunciation, but, along with the above-mentioned regional-accent problem, there's the fact that amateur teachers might give incorrect advice.

Pronouncing Italian words

Italian is a purely phonetic language, which means that the pronunciation is always consistent with the spelling, with nearly no exceptions. This means that, unlike English where the same group of letters can have different pronunciations (bow, bow, dough, cough etc.), in Italian the pronunciation stays the same:

Gatto (cat) = *Gaat-toh*
Ratto (rat) = *Raat-toh*
Baratto (barter) = *Baa-raat-toh*
Fontana (fountain) = *Phon-taa-na*
Montana (mountain-related) = *Mon-taa-na*
Lontana (far) = *Lon-taa-na*

The only exception to this rule, besides those foreign words that entered the Italian dictionary, are words that only differ in a graphic or tonic accent (we'll explain this in a short while).

Pronunciation of the Italian letters

The modern Italian alphabet consists of the same 26 letters we have in English. In the past century, it used to have only 21 letters and J, K, W, X, and Y were not part of it. These letters were added when the use of foreign words in Italian became consistent, and most words containing these letters are originally not Italian, with few exceptions.

As Italian is a phonetic language, letters are the main factor concurring to the overall pronunciation. Some Italian letters are pronounced just like in English, while others have a different pronunciation. Let's see what this is all about in the following table:

(In the table, graphic and tonic accents are mentioned. If you don't know what they are, skip the table and get back to it after reading the paragraph about phonetic accents, which is right after this table.)

Letter	Letter name	Pronunciation	Examples
A	A - *Ah*	Always like the "a" in far, car, bar	Amore (*aa-moh-reh* - love) Arte (*ar-teh* - art) Antico (*ahn-tee-ko* - ancient)
B	Bi or b - *Bee or bh*	Always like English	Bacio (*baa-tchoh* - kiss) Buono (*boo-oh-noh* - good) Bello (*bel-loh* - nice)
C	Ci or c - *Tchee or kh*	The pronunciation depends on what follows. C + "i" or "e" makes a tchee/tcheh sound as in cheese or chew. C + "i" + vowel also makes a tch' sound, and in this case the I is silent. In all the other cases (C + consonant or H or "a", "o", "u") it is a kh sound as in club or kart.	Ciao (*tchaaoh* - hello/bye) Cena (*tcheh-nah* - dinner) Crosta (*kroh-stah* - crust) Chiesa (*kee-eh-sah* - church) Casa (*kaa-sah* - home/house)
D	Di or d - *Dee or dh*	Always like English	Dente (*den-teh* - tooth) Dieci (*dee-eh-tchee* - ten) Dentista (*den-tee-stah* -

			dentist)
E	E - *Eh*	This letter can be pronounced as a close/high vowel, like the "e" in pen, or an open/low vowel, like the "e" in eight. When there's a graphic accent, the close "e" is spelled "è", while the open "e" is spelled "é". This being said, this difference in pronunciation varies across regional accents, so don't worry about getting it wrong, as most Italians also get it wrong.	E (*éh* - and) È (*èh* - is) Elfo (*èlf-oh* - elf) Europa (*éh-oo-roh-pah* - Europe) Pesca (*pés-kah* - fishing (noun)) Pesca (*pès-kah* - peach) N.B. In this one case, we chose to add tonic accents (see below the table) to the transliteration. This will not be done regularly.
F	Effe or f - *Ef-feh (or fh)*	Always like English	Forum (*pho-room* - forum) Foto (*pho-toh* - photo) Forchetta (*phor-ket-tah* - fork)
G	Gi or g - *Jee (or gh)*	Definitely the hardest letter in Italian. The pronunciation depends on what follows. In most cases, this letter makes the same "gh" sound it makes in English, but not when it's followed by the letter I, E, L or N. G + I or E makes a "dj" sound, as in jeep or gym. When it's a G + I + A/O cluster, the I is basically silent, and it only indicates that the G has to be pronounced "dj"	Gatto (*gaat-toh* - cat) Grotta (*grot-tah* - cave) Gioco (*djoh-koh* - game) Ghianda (*ghee-aan-dah* - acorn) Generale (*djeh-neh-raa-leh* - general) Ghepardo (*gheh-par-doh* - cheetah) Gnu (*'nyoo* - wildebeest) Gnocchi (*'nyok-kee* - gnocchi) Gnomo (*'nyo-moh* - gnome) Glicine (*glee-tchee-neh* - wisteria)

		and not "gh". G + N and G + L are the most complicated sounds, as they do not exist in English. In the phonetic alphabet, the G + N sound is spelled 'ɲ; it sounds like the Spanish ñ and resembles the "nee"/"nyo" sound in onion; we'll transliterate the sound as -'nee or 'nyo. When the combination is within a word, G + L + I make a sound that is spelled ʎ in IPA and is basically a stronger version of the Spanish LL, like in "pollo"; it resembles the English y in year, and we'll transliterate the sound as - 'y. When the G + L combination is at the beginning of a word, it is pronounced like in English, with the only exception of the article "gli" ('yee), and its composite forms.	Globo (*gloh-boh* - globe) Gli (*'yee* - the) Coniglio (*koh-nee-'yoh* - rabbit) Foglio (*foh-'yoh* - sheet) Maglia (*maa-'yah* - t-shirt)
H	Acca - *Ak-kah*	In Italian the letter H is always silent and mostly used in combination with C and G as seen before, or in foreign words.	Hotel (*oh-tel* - hotel) Hall (*all* - hall) Ho (*òh* - I have) O (*óh* - or) Hanno (*an-noh* - they have) Anno (*an-noh* - year) Chi (*kee* - who)

I	I - *Ee*	The letter I is always pronounced like the "e" in "me", but sometimes it is practically silent, especially when it's a CI or GI + vowel.	Indicazioni (*een-dee-kaa-tzeeoh-nee* - indications) Imbarco (*eem-bar-koh* - boarding) Già (*geeàh* - already)
J	Gei or I lunga (long I) - *Jay or Ee Loon-gah*	It's pronounced just like the Italian I, except for foreign words.	Juventus (*eeoo-vent-oos* - juventus) Jugoslavia (*eeoo-goh-slah-veeah* - yugoslavia) Jacuzzi (*eeaa-kootz-tzee* - Jacuzzi) Jeep (*djeep* - jeep) Jet (*djet* - jet) Judo (*djoo-doh* - judo)
K	Cappa - *Kap-pah*	Always like English	KO (*kaap-paa-òh* - KO) Kitsch (*kee-tch* - kitsch) Killer (*keel-ler* - killer)
L	Elle or l - *El-leh or lh*	Always like English	Lungo (*loon-go* - long) Luce (*loo-tche* - light) Letto (*leht-toh* - bed)
M	Emme or m - *Em-meh or mh*	Always like English	Mano (*maa-noh* - hand) Maschio (*maas-kyo* - male) Mulo (*moo-loh* - mule)
N	Enne or n - *En-neh or nh*	Always like English (except for the "gn" combination)	Nuvola (*noo-voh-lah* - cloud) Nuovo (*noo-oh-voh* - new) Notte (*not-teh* - night)
O	O - *Oh*	This letter can be pronounced as a close/high vowel, like the "o" in lost, or an open/low vowel, like the "o" in cold.	Oblò (*oh-blòh* - porthole) Otto (*ot-toh* - eight) Ombra (*om-brah* - shadow)

P	Pi or p - *Pee or p-uh*	Always like English	Pagare (*paa-gah-reh* - to pay) Pane (*paa-neh* - bread) Partenze (*paar-ten-zeh* - departures)
Q	Q - *Koo*	Normally followed by U, it always has a K sound.	Quaglia (*kwaa-'yah* - quail) Quinto (*kwin-toh* - fifth) Acqua (*aak-kwah* - water)
R	Erre or r - *Er-reh or rh*	The Italian R is always rolled, but not as much as in Spanish.	Rubare (*roo-baa-reh* - to steal) Ricordare (*ree-kor-daa-reh* - to remember) Rompere (*rom-peh-reh* - to break)
S	Esse or s - *Es-seh or suh*	The sound is similar to English, but in some cases it sounds in-between an S and a Z.	Sono (*Soh-noh* - I am) Sonno (*Son-noh* - sleep) Sapere (*Saa-peh-reh* - to know)
T	Ti or t - *Tee or tuh*	Always like British English	Tutto (*toot-toh* - everything) Tasse (*taas-seh* - taxes) Tuo (*too-oh* - your)
U	U - *Uh*	The letter U is always pronounced like the "oo" in "too".	Uccello (*ootch-tchel-loh* - bird) Unicorno (*oo-nee-kor-noh* - unicorn) Uno (*oo-noh* - one)
V	Vi or vu or v - *Vee or voo or vh*	Always like English	Visto (*vees-toh* - visa) Vuoto (*voo-oh-toh* - empty) Valore (*vaa-loh-reh* - value)
W	Vu doppia	Only foreign words have	W.C. (*vee-tchee* - W.C.)

	or doppiavu (double v) - *Voo dop-peeah or dop-peeaa-voo*	W's and the pronunciation usually depends on the original language and can be a V sound like in vase or a W sound as in Washington.	Wafer (*vaa-fehr* - wafer) Watt (*vaat* - watt) Wow (*oo-aa-oo* - wow) Wasabi (*ooaa-saa-bee* - wasabi) Web (*ooeb* - web)
X	Ics - *eex*	Always like English	Xenofobia (*kseh-noh-foh-bee-ah* - xenophobia) Xilofono (*ksee-loh-foh-noh* - xylophone) Xeno (*kseh-noh* - xenon)
Y	Ipsilon or I greca (greek I) - Ee-psee-lon or ee greh-ka	Always like English	Yogurt (*yo-goort* - yogurt) Yo-yo (*yò-yò* - yo-yo) Yeti (*yeh-tee* - yeti)
Z	Zeta or z - *dzeh-ta or zh*	Always pronounced like "ts" or "dz", with regional variability between the two.	Pazzo (*pat-tsoh* - mad man) Alzare (*al-tsa-reh* - to lift) Zizzania (*dzeed-dzaa-nee-ah* - discord)

DOUBLE CONSONANTS

One of the most difficult parts in pronouncing Italian words for native English speakers is getting the double consonants right. Many Italian words have double consonants, so it's a frequent issue. Some letters make a sound that can be prolonged (all vowels and some consonants like F, R, S, and maybe just a couple more), but in most cases you can't just make the sound longer. So, how do you do it? There are two ways to approach this; let's take the word "tutto" (all, everything) as an example:

1. Make the sound twice. Pronounce tutto like *toot-toh*. [This is the transliteration we'll be using in this book, for simplicity of reading.]
2. Make a pause before the consonant. Pronounce tutto like too-'-toh.

Which works best? Probably a combination of the two. Either one can be the solution, depending on the specific speaker's difficulties.

Phonetic accents

Accents indicate what letter (always a vowel) you have to stress when pronouncing a word. There are two types of accents:

A <u>graphic accent</u> is an accent you can read, meaning that it's always written, and in Italian it is always on the last vowel of a word:

Pero (pear tree) = *Peh-roh*
Però (but, however) = *Peh-ròh*
Faro (lighthouse) = *Fah-roh*
Farò (I will do) = *Fah-ròh*

A <u>tonic accent</u>, or pitch accent, is an accent that is normally not written, and is on a vowel that's not the last one of the word:

Ancora (again) = *Aan-<u>kòh</u>-ra*
Ancora (anchor) = <u>*Àan*</u>*-koh-ra*
Ambito (scope, ambit) = <u>*Àam*</u>*-bee-toh*
Ambito (longed for, target of desire and ambition) = *Aam-<u>béé</u>-toh*

In this case, it is impossible to tell which word is which, out of context. In this book, we will not specify where the tonic accent is, not at all times, because it might be mistaken for a different accent and get confusing for a beginner. If you have available the audiobook version of this book, you can always use it to have confirmation of what part of the word is to be stressed.

Take-home message

This first lesson was probably a bit of a shock, but don't worry, it just takes time. Future lessons will be much lighter, on average at least. You will see that different lessons take different amounts of time to be digested, so you can take the chance to go back to an older lesson when the new one doesn't take up all your time.

This chapter can be a great first approach to Italian pronunciation, but it is not advisable to study this subject without including audio and video material in your learning plan. Using the audiobook version of this book can be an easy solution.

When you pronounce a word in Italian, try to center your focus on the hardest letter, especially C, G, O, and E, and on double consonants. Once you master that portion, you can start worrying about accent and cadence. What is most important, though, is not to be shy, and practice as often as you can, pronouncing the words out loud, on your own or with a partner.

0.2
Vocabulary and False Friends

Building up vocabulary is one of the hardest parts of learning a language because it's something you have to learn by heart, and there are very few ways to get around it. The best recommendation to achieve a solid vocabulary is to expose yourself to the language as much as you can, possibly in a friendly and motivating environment, like your favorite TV shows.

This book will not present you with a never-ending list of nouns and verbs, which will probably not only be daunting but also useless, as you would only retain a very small percentage of that information. Also, smartphones have proper dictionaries, so there's no need for an incomplete one in this book.

Instead, we will work on a small amount of new vocabulary at a time, around a dozen words per lesson, and have you focus on those.

Building up vocabulary

Vocabulary is clearly necessary in order to speak a language, so you will have to build up your personal vocabulary, word after word. This crucial process can take a lot of time, which makes it especially important to find the best solutions to get the major profit with the minor effort.

Generally speaking, the best thing to do is diversifying the learning sources, for example by complementing this book with some video material (e.g. movies and TV shows with subtitles) and/or simplified novels for learners. It might be a good idea to keep a physical or virtual notebook with you as you go through this process, to take down notes when necessary.

Along with hard work, there are a few tricks that can help overcome vocabulary issues.

If you don't know a word that you want to USE, you can find a synonym or try and phrase the sentence differently. Otherwise, you can try and make up a word that sounds Italian starting from an English word of Latin derivation; you might be lucky. However, considering that nowadays most people have a virtual dictionary in their pockets, it is not easy to think of a situation where that would be the best option.

If you don't know a word , and you want to UNDER-STAND it, you have many more options, especially if you see it written. If you hear it, there are too many variables, including the fact that your brain and memory might mess things up, or that you might not know how to spell it; in this case, the best way to go is to record the word for future search, if you're hearing it from an audio or video source, or tell the speaker that you don't know the word, if it's a real-life situation. When the word is written, etymology can come and help you. Many English words have root words in common with their Italian cognates, so, even when you're a complete beginner, it should not be so hard to notice the link. For example, if you find an uncommon word like "annichilire" (*aan-nee-kee-lee-reh*), you might still be lucky enough to notice the link with "to annihilate".

False friends

The strategy we just described finds its mortal enemy in false friends. A false friend is a word that seems to be "friendly", meaning that it looks like an English word , and so you think you are able to translate it easily, but it actually has a very different meaning than the English twin-word. A simple example can be the Italian word "caldo" (*kahl-doh*). It's a common word even for beginners, and you can find it on water taps, thermostats, and various types of machinery. Considering the context, many people would reasonably think it means "cold", as it resembles the English word, but truth is it actually means "hot". These words might trick you in believing they have a certain meaning, when they actually have a different one.

Even though the two languages are not phonetically very similar, there's an incredible amount of Italian words that might remind of English words but mean something different. There are even cases in which the word is actually the same, but the meaning is not. Let's see some examples.

Italian Word	Meaning	False Friend	False Friend's Translation
Annoiare	To bore	to Annoy	Infastidire
Argomento	Topic	Argument	Discussione
Attualmente	Currently	Actually	In realtà
Box	Garage	Box	Scatola
Camera	Room	Camera	Fotocamera
Carro	Carriage	Car	Automobile
Casuale	Random	Casual	Informale

Collegio	Boarding School	College	Università
Comprensivo	Understanding	Comprehen-sive	Esauriente
Consistente	Solid or Significant	Consistent	Costante or Coerente
Convenienza	Affordability	Convenience	Comodità
Educato	Well-mannered	Educated	Istruito
Estate	Summer	Estate	Proprietà
Eventual-mente	In case	Eventually	Alla fine
Fattoria	Farm	Factory	Industria
Fornitura	Supply	Furniture	Mobili
Largo	Wide	Large	Grosso
Libreria	Bookshop	Library	Biblioteca
Lunatico	Moody	Lunatic	Pazzo
Lussuria	Lust	Luxury	Lusso
Magazzino	Warehouse	Magazine	Rivista
Mansione	Task or Duty	Mansion	Villa
Morbido	Soft or Mellow	Morbid	Morboso
Parente	Relative	Parent	Genitore
Pavimento	Floor	Pavement (sidewalk)	Marciapiedi
Petrolio	Oil	Petrol	Benzina
Preservativo	Condom	Preservative	Conservante
Pretendere	To demand	To pretend	Fingere

Rumore	Noise	Rumor	Pettegolezzo
Spot	Commercial	Spot	Macchia
Ultimo	Last	Ultimate	Definitivo

The whole list is actually much longer than this, but we made a selection of the words that are most useful for beginners.

Take-home message

The best and easiest way to learn vocabulary is to expose yourself to Italian content or to an Italian environment, while having this false-friend list always with you to avoid misunderstandings. Don't rush into learning random words from a dictionary, just experience something you like in Italian, a game or TV show for example, and you'll learn thousands of words effortlessly.

0.3
Basics of Italian grammar

Italian grammar is a huge and complex topic, and we will only start to skim it in this book. We want you to have the basic tools to make your first experiences with Italian, without boring you to death. As you advance in your studies, you'll start to complete the puzzle, and you will be willing to dig deeper into grammar.

This is going to be another lengthy chapter, so we suggest doing the same as with pronunciation and come back to this chapter on days when you finish the daily chapter in little time.

Considering that Italian grammar is particularly complex, especially in comparison with English, you might want to quickly review your English grammar knowledge, to make sure you're familiar with simple terms like noun, subject, direct object, adverb, clause, etc.

The focus of this section will be nouns and articles, which are the best starting point. We will briefly touch on the other elements and structures, but this book is not primarily focused on grammar, so we will set aside those topics for later on. This series of books ("Learn Italian For Adult Beginners") will include a volume about grammar specifically [see "suggested readings" in our conclusive chapter], so we entrust you to the other title of this collection for what concerns the other grammar topics.

Nouns

The particularity of Italian nouns is that they differ in gender as well as in number. A word can be singular or plural (singolare e plurale, *seen-goh-laa-reh eh ploo-raa-leh*) but also masculine or feminine (maschile e femminile, *maas-kee-leh e fem-mee-nee-leh*).

This could be rather irrelevant, besides grammar, with words like ombrello (*ohm-brehl-loh* - umbrella). On the contrary, in other cases the gender can be informative, for example with animals, where "il gatto" is a male cat and "la gatta" is a female cat.

Unfortunately, the reasons why a word is masculine or feminine are not very consistent, but the ending of the word can usually indicate which it is.

GENDER

There are general rules about the gender (genere - *djeh-neh-reh*) and number (numero - *noo-meh-roh*) of Italian nouns, but unfortunately there are exceptions.

Most commonly, masculine words end in -o in the singular and -i in the plural, while feminine words end respectively in -a and -e (be careful that -e ending words can sometimes be masculine singular or feminine singular, as we will see in a minute).

NUMBER

As for the number, all Italian words are countable, even though some words can be used like uncountable words are used in English. Very few words don't have a plural (or singular) version, and they are usually not a problem for learners; you won't need to use the plural of those, even without knowing that it doesn't exist.

Please note that all foreign words should always be used in the singular in Italian (un jet → due jet, un hotel → due hotel, uno smartphone → due smartphone), even though people tend to forget this rule when it's words that only recently started to be used consistently.

GENDER AND NUMBER RULES

There are two basic sets of rules for gender and number, plus many exceptions to these rules. Let's summarize them in the following tables:

+	Singolare	Plurale	Examples
Maschile	**-o**	**-i**	Amico (*aa-mee-koh*) → Amici (*aa-mee-tchee)* = friend(s) Bacio (*baa-tchoh*) → Baci (*baa-tchee*) = kiss(es) Costo (*cost-oh*) → Costi (*cost-ee*) = cost(s) Dado (*dah-doh*) → Dadi (*dah-dee*) = die/dice Esso (*ehs-soh*) → Essi (*ehs-see*) = it/them Fatto (*faat-toh*) → Fatti (*faat-tee*) = fact(s)
Femminile	**-a**	**-e**	Gondola (*gon-doh-lah*) → Gondole (*gon-doh-leh*) = gondola(s) Isola (*ee-sol-ah*) → Isole (*ee-sol-eh*) = island(s) Lama (*lah-mah*) → Lame (*lah-meh*) = blade(s) Mora (*moh-rah*) → More (*moh-reh*) = blackberry(-ies) Nota (*noh-tah*) → Note (*noh-teh*) = note(s) Ora (*oh-rah*) → Ore (*oh-reh*) = hour(s)

Although this is the standard rule, there are exceptions. For example, the word lama (la lama = the blade) can also mean llama, but in this case it is masculine (il lama; the spelling doesn't change) and the plural is also lama (i lama; still masculine and same spelling).

There is a second set of rules, for words that in the singular end in -e. These words can be either masculine or feminine.

	Singolare	Plurale	Examples
Maschile	-e	-i	il cane (ka-neh) → i cani (ka-nee) = dog(s) il padre (pah-dreh) → i padri (pah-dree) = father(s) il mare (mah-reh) → i mari (mah-ree) = sea(s)
Femminile	-e	-i	la prigione (pree-djoh-neh) → le prigioni (pree-djoh-nee) = prison(s) la madre (mah-dreh) → le m adri (mah-dree) = mother(s) la nave (nah-veh) → le navi (nah-vee) = ship(s)

There are also irregular words that don't follow any of these rules, but fortunately they're not many. For example, words like papà (*pah-pàh*) or caffè (*kuf-fèh*) are identical in the singular and plural.

Other words can even change gender, like the word uovo (l'uovo - *woh-voh*), egg, which is masculine in the singular and becomes feminine, uova (le uova - *woh-vah*) in the plural, and ends in an -a.

Finally, there are words that "pretend" to have a different gender, like mano (la mano - *mah-noh*), plural mani (le mani - *mah-nee*), which seems to follow the classic rule for masculine nouns but is actually feminine.

These wildly irregular ones are a very small minority of words.

Now that I have scared and confused you enough, let's talk about one of the greatest helpers in figuring gender and number out: the article.

Articles

Italian nouns are almost always preceded by an article, both in the plural and in the singular form, and regardless of the sentence structure or the presence of prepositions.

In Italian, there are two sets of articles. The "articoli determinativi" (*ar-tee-koh-lee det-er-mee-nah-tee-vee*), or definite articles, are used for an identified noun and are similar to the English "the". The "articoli indeterminativi" (*ar-tee-koh-lee een-det-er-mee-nah-tee-vee*), or indefinite articles, are used for an unidentified noun and are similar to the English "a/an/some".

ARTICOLI DETERMINATIVI

Feminine articles are easier and work as follows:

Used before:	Singular	Plural	Examples
words starting in any consonant	la	le	La lama (*lah lah-mah*) → Le lame (*leh lah-meh*) = the blade(s) La mora (*moh-rah*) → Le more (*moh-reh*) = the blackberry(-ies) La nota (*noh-tah*) → Le note (*noh-teh*) = the note(s)
words starting in any vowel	l'	le	L'isola (*lh ee-sol-ah*) → Le isole (*leh ee-sol-eh*) = the island(s) L'ora (*oh-rah*) → Le ore (*oh-reh*) = the hour(s) L'amica (*ah-mee-kah*) → Le amiche (*ah-mee-keh*) = the (female) friend(s)

Masculine articles are a little trickier:

Used before:	Singular	Plural	Examples
words starting in most consonants	**il**	**i**	Il costo (*eel cost-oh*) → I costi (*ee cost-ee*) = the cost(s) Il dado (*dah-doh*) → I dadi (*dah-dee*) = the die/dice Il fatto (*fat-toh*) → I fatti (*fat-tee*) = the fact(s)
words starting in a proper vowel	**l'**	**gli**	L'amico (*lh ah-mee-koh*) → Gli amici (*'yee ah-mee-tchee*) = the friend(s) L'esorcista (*ehs-sohr-tchee-stah*) → Gli esorcisti (*ehs-sohr-tchee-stee*) = the exorcist(s) L'atto (*aht-toh*) → Gli atti (*aht-tee*) = the act(s)
words starting in: GN PS PN S + consonant Y Z	**lo**	**gli**	Lo gnocco (*loh 'nyok-koh*) → Gli gnocchi (*'yee 'nyok-kee*) = the gnocchi (conuntable in IT) Lo psichiatra (*psee-kee-ah-trah*) → Gli psichiatri (*psee-kee-ah-tree*) = the psychiatrist(s) Lo pneumatico (*pneh-oo-maht-ee-koh*) → Gli pneumatici (*pneh-oo-maht-ee-tchee*) = the tire(s) Lo scudo (*skoo-doh*) → Gli scudi (*skoo-dee*) = the shield(s) Lo yougurt (*yo-goor-t*) → Gli yogurt (*yo-goor-t*) = the yogurt (countable in IT) Lo zoo (*dz-oh-oh*) → Gli zoo (*dz-oh-oh*) = the zoo(s)

The - l' - article, be it masculine or feminine, is just a shorter version of lo/la (l'isola = la isola, l'amico = lo amico), and it is technically not incorrect to use the longer article, although nobody does it unless it's necessary.

Definite articles can also merge with prepositions and form the so-called "articulated prepositions", which we will mention later.

ARTICOLI INDETERMINATIVI

Indefinite articles are used for things that are being mentioned in general or that are being presented now and had not been mentioned before.

Once again, the feminine versions are easier:

Used before:	Singular	Plural	Examples
words starting in any consonant	**una**	**delle**	Una lama (*oo-nah lah-mah*) → Delle lame (*dehl-leh lah-meh*) = a blade/some blades Una mora (*moh-rah*) → Delle more (*moh-reh*) = a blackberry/some blackbarries Una nota (*noh-tah*) → Delle note (*noh-teh*) = a note/some notes
words starting in any vowel	**un'**	**delle**	Un'isola (*oon ee-sol-ah*) → Delle isole (*dehl-leh ee-sol-eh*) = an island/some islands Un'ora (*oh-rah*) → Delle ore (*oh-reh*) = an hour/some hours Un'amica (*ah-mee-kah*) → Delle amiche (*ah-mee-keh)* = a/some (female) friend/friends

28

Here as well, masculine articles are a little trickier:

Used before:	Singular	Plural	Examples
words starting in most consonants	**un**	**dei**	Un costo (*oon cost-oh*) → Dei costi (*day cost-ee*) = a cost/some costs Un dado (*dah-doh*) → Dei dadi (*dah-dee*) = a die/some dice Un fatto (*fat-toh*) → Dei fatti (*fat-tee*) = a fact/some facts
words starting in a proper vowel	**un**	**degli**	Un amico (*oon ah-mee-koh*) → degli amici (*deh-'yee ah-mee-tchee*) = a friend/some friends Un esorcista (*ehs-sohr-tchee-stah*) → Degli esorcisti (*ehs-sohr-tchee-stee*) = a maleexorcist/some exorcists Un atto (*aht-toh*) → degli atti (*aht-tee*) = an act/some acts
words starting in: GN PS PN S + consonant Y Z	**uno**	**degli**	Uno gnocco (*oon-oh 'nyok-koh*) → Degli gnocchi (*deh-'yee 'nyok-kee*) = some gnocchi (countable in IT) Uno psichiatra (*psee-kee-ah-trah*) → Degli psichiatri (*psee-kee-ah-tree*) = a psychiatrist/some psychiatrists Uno pneumatico (*pneh-oo-maht-ee-koh*) → Degli pneumatici (*pneh-oo-maht-ee-tchee*) = a tire/some tires Uno scudo (*skoo-doh*) → Degli scudi (*skoo-dee*) = a shield/some shields Uno yogurt (*yo-goor-t*) → Degli yogurt (*yo-goor-t*) = some yogurt (countable in IT) Uno zoo (*dz-oh-oh*) → Degli zoo (*dz-oh-oh*) = a zoo/some zoos

Take-home message

Italian grammar is a dense topic, and it's best not to overdo it because it can be demotivating. Unfortunately, you cannot completely ignore it, so take it in small pills and try to enjoy the best of it, like the ways in which grammar adds detail and specificity to the words.

From this first grammar lesson, just take home what is essential. Remember how to tell whether a regular noun is masculine or feminine and singular or plural, and remember the basic articles, especially since they can usually help you in that.

All the rest will come back to you when it's time.

0.4
Basics of Italian grammar, part 2

At this point, you're probably still trying to digest your first grammar lesson, which is the hardest lesson you will find in this book. Conscious of that, this next chapter will be much lighter and shorter. Today we will just quickly mention all the remaining grammatical elements and structures, giving you just the key points to set the basis for your future learning.

Let's get going!

Adjectives

Italian adjectives have to follow the basic rule of "agreeing" in gender and number with the noun they modify. For example, "beautiful houses", needing to use bello (*behl-loh*) for beautiful and casa (*cah-dsah*) for house, is going to be "belle case", with bello being used in the feminine plural version: "belle".

There are no adjectives with irregular plurals or anything like that, so all you have to do is figure out the number and gender of the noun they modify, and adapt the adjective consequently, choosing between -o, -a, -i, and -e as an ending.

Let's now quickly take a look at the possessive adjectives:

Possessive adjectives	
My	Mio
Your	Tuo
His	Suo
Her	Suo
Its	Suo
Our	Nostro
Your	Vostro
Their	Loro

It's not important now that you remember all these; just read them a couple of times , and then you can come back to this table when you encounter them in the future.

Verbs

Verbs are probably the hardest part of Italian grammar, having 3 conjugations, 7 moods, up to 8 tenses, and considering the existence of many irregular verbs. For the moment, we'll just describe the main types of verbs.

CLASSIFICATION

There are 2 main ways to classify verbs: by the ending, and by the grammatical structures that follow.

Italian infinitive verbs have 3 possible endings: -are, -ere, and -ire. These are, respectively, the first, second, and third Italian conjugations. All verbs fall under one of these categories, and follow category-specific conjugation rules.

Verbs can also be classified as transitive and intransitive, depending on whether they can (→ transitive) or cannot (→ intransitive) be followed by a direct object.

CONJUGATION

Italian conjugations are divided into 2 groups, 7 "moods" (modi - *moh-dee*) and 8 tenses (tempi - *tem-pee*), but most moods don't have all 8 tenses. In this first table, we'll see all these moods and learn what they're used for.

Group	Mood	Use
Modi finiti (*moh-dee phee-nee-tee*) Finite moods	**Indicativo**	Used to describe an actual event, it's the main mood in most languages.
	Congiuntivo	Used to describe an opinion or an uncertain event.
	Condizionale	Used to describe an event that is under a certain condition.
	Imperativo*	Used to give orders.
Modi indefiniti (*moh-dee een-deh-phee-nee-tee*) Indefinite moods	**Gerundio**	Used to describe a consideration.
	Participio	It's the verb being used as a noun or adjective.
	Infinito	Infinitive, like in English.

* the Imperativo mood is identical to Indicativo in most cases (and usually just rendered with an exclamation mark); only a

handful of verbs have a separate conjugation. Also, only the second-person singular and plural (A.K.A. "you") exist.

Let's now take a look at the 8 tenses in the various moods (spoiler: only Indicativo has all 8); we'll take the verb "to buy", comprare (*kom-praa-reh*), as an example, just to give you an idea of how it works. Comprare is a regular verb of the first-conjugation group (-are). We will be conjugating it in the first person only.

Mood	Tense	Used to describe an action that...	Example
Indicativo	**Presente**	happens in the present	Compro (*kom-proh*) I buy
	Passato prossimo	just happened and still affects the present	Ho comprato (*oh kom-praa-toh*) I have bought
	Imperfetto	was continuous in the past	Compravo (*kom-praa-voh*) I was buying
	Trapassato prossimo	was continuous in a further-back past	Avevo comprato (*aa-veh-voh kom-praa-toh*) I had been buying
	Passato remoto	happened in the past and doesn't significantly affect the present	Comprai (*kom-praa-ee*) I bought
	Trapassato remoto	happened in a further-back past and doesn't significantly affect the present	Ebbi comprato (*ehb-bee kom-praa-toh*) I had bought

	Futuro semplice	will happen	Comprerò (*kom-preh-ròh*)
			I will buy or I am going to buy
	Futuro anteriore	will have happened	Avrò comprato (*aa-vròh kom-prah-toh*)
			I will have bought
Congiuntivo	**Presente**	is uncertain in the present	(che io) Compri ((*keh eeoh*) *kom-pree*)
			(should I) buy,
	Passato	was uncertain in the past	(che io) Abbia comprato (*aab-bee-ah kom-praa-toh*)
			(should I) have bought,
	Imperfetto	was uncertain and continuous in the past	(che io) Comprassi (*kom-praas-see*)
			Had I bought,
	Trapassato	was uncertain and continuous in a further-back past	(che io) Avessi comprato (*aa-vehs-see kom-praa-toh*)
			Had I (had) bought
Condizionale	**Presente**	would happen under a certain condition	Comprerei (*kom-preh-reh-ee*)
			I would buy

	Passato	would have happened under a certain condition	Avrei comprato (*aa-vreh-ee kom-prah-toh*)
			I would have bought
Imperativo	**Presente**	must happen	Compra! (*kom-prah!*)
			Buy!
	Presente	sets a condition	Comprando (*kom-praan-doh*)
			By buying
Gerundio	**Passato**	set a condition	Avendo comprato (*aa-vehn-doh kom-praa-toh*)
			By having bought
Mood	**Tense**	**Used to...**	**Example**
Participio	**Presente**	describe the doer of the action	Comprante (*kom-praan-teh*)
			He who buys
	Passato	describe the doer of a past action	Avente comprato (*aa-vehn-teh kom-praa-toh*)
			He who bought
Infinito	**Presente**	describe an action	Comprare (*kom-praa-reh*)
			To buy
	Passato	describe a past action	Avere comprato (*aa-veh-reh kom-praa-toh*)
			To have bought

In addition to these conjugations, in Italian you can mimic the English present and past continuous by using the verb stare (*stah-reh*), which means "to stay" or "to be (physically)", followed by a verb in the Gerundio tense. For example, I am buying is translated: "Io sto comprando" (*eeoh stoh kom-praa-ndoh*).

Prepositions

There are 9 simple prepositions (preposizioni semplici) and some of them can merge with articles to create articled prepositions (preposizioni articolate). Let's take a look at the table:

Italian **<u>simple</u> preposition**	English preposition
Di	Of
A	To
Da	From
In	In
Con	With
Su	On
Per	For
Tra	Among, between, in
Fra	Among, between, in

Unfortunately, a substantial amount of prepositions are not used in the same way as in English and there's not always logic behind the choice of the preposition, in either language. You'll just know which to use from experience.

Let's just quickly see what articled prepositions are:

Preposizioni articolate						
+	**il**	**lo**	**la**	**i**	**gli**	**le**
di	del	dello	della	dei	degli	delle
a	al	allo	alla	ai	agli	alle
da	dal	dallo	dalla	dai	dagli	dalle
in	nel	nello	nella	nei	negli	nelle
con	col	-	-	coi	-	-
su	sul	sullo	sulla	sui	sugli	sulle

Ok, they exist, make peace with it. A beginner should probably not start worrying about these for the first year or so, hence this problematic task is for the future you. Let's move on to pronouns!

Pronouns

It's time to take a look at the main types of Italian pronouns; we'll cover personal pronouns and possessive pronouns in the following table.

Subjective pronouns		Objective pronouns		Possessive pronouns*	
I	**Io**	Me	**Me/Mi**	Mine	**Mi-o/a/ei/e**
You	**Tu**	You	**Te/Ti**	Yours	**Tu-o/a/oi/e**
He	**Lui/Egli**	Him	**Lo/Gli**	His	**Su-o/a/oi/e**

She	Lei/Ella	Her	La/Le	Hers	Su-o/a/oi/e
It	Esso/Essa	It	Lo/Gli	Its	Su-o/a/oi/e
We	Noi	Us	Noi/Ci	Ours	Nostr-o/a/i/e
You	Voi	You	Voi/Vi	Yours	Vostr-o/a/i/e
They	Essi	Them	Loro/Gli	Theirs	Loro

* these pronouns have to agree in gender and number with the noun they substitute or modify, which is why there are 4 possible endings, as seen with adjectives.

Italian wording and structure

In this final part of the grammar section, we'll describe the general workings of Italian sentences.

The usual sentence structure consists of subject, verb and object, with all the other complements orbiting around this trio. One peculiarity of the Italian language is that the subject can usually be omitted, purposely or if unnecessary, as the verb conjugation already gives information about the subject. The order is usually *subject, verb, object*, as in:

Marco ha una mela.

Ha una mela.

(*Mark-oh ah oo-nah meh-lah*)

(*Ah oo-nah meh-lah*)

Marco has an apple.

(He/she/it) has an apple.

39

It is however possible to invert the order by modifying the sentence, as it is possible in English, maybe with just a little more flexibility.

WORDING QUESTIONS

In Italian, questions have the same construction and word order as a statement, with a question mark at the end. As simple as that. Let's see the same example:

1. Marco ha una mela.
2. Marco ha una mela?

1. (*Mark-oh ah oo-nah meh-lah*)
2. (*Mark-oh ah oo-nah meh-lah?*)

1. Marco has an apple.
2. Does Marco have an apple?

At this point, you're probably wondering how this is possible. When it's written, ok, there's the question mark. But how can I tell whether I'm being asked a question or listening to a statement? And how can I ask a question and not make a statement?

Well, it's a combination of factors. First and foremost, during a conversation you can usually understand from the content whether it is a question or a statement. Secondly, people usually have a different intonation when asking a question. Last but not least, after asking their question, they would probably pause and stare at you waiting for an answer. With all this being said, it is still possible to misunderstand and "is that a question or a statement?" is something you hear quite often in Italian.

This closes our quick overview of Italian grammar.

Take-home message

Don't worry about grammar too much for now, just throw yourself into Italian, dive in for a full immersion, and possibly find someone with whom you can practice; there are plenty of communities for that. The time for grammar will come.

You can't expect to learn grammar in one shot anyway. This chapter was only meant to introduce you to the whole of the topic, and there's nothing on which you have to focus specifically, for the time being. So, move on, move to things you like. You'll get back to grammar and these tables when a situation calls for it, and that's the way it should work; it's the most efficient and sustainable way.

If this book was not your first experience with Italian, and you feel like you already want to know more about Italian grammar, we recommend reading the second book of this series:

"Italian Workbook For Adult Beginners: Speak Italian in 30 Days!: Learn Italian Grammar & Vocabulary with Lessons, Activities, and Fun Exercises"

0.5
Let's Practice!

This first series of exercises will let you practice with what you have learned so far. This session will consist of a pronunciation part and a grammar part.

Pronunciation exercises

1) Find the correct transcription for the word "Mela". What does this word mean?

   A. Mee-lah
   B. Meh-lah
   C. Me-ya

2) Find the correct transcription for the word "Passaporto". What does this word mean?

   A. Pass-ah-por-tou
   B. Pas-app-ort-oh
   C. Pahs-sah-por-toh

3) Find the correct transcription for the word "Automobile". What does this word mean?

   A. Oh-toh-moh-bee-leh
   B. Ah-oo-toh-moh-by-lh
   C. Ah-oo-toh-moh-bee-leh

4) Find the correct transcription for the word "Chiesa". What does this word mean?

A. Kee-eh-sah
B. Tchee-eh-sa
C. Hee-eh-sa

5) Find the correct transcription for the word "Gnomo". What does this word mean?

A. Gnoh-moh
B. Nee-oh-moh
C. 'nyo-moh

6) Find the correct transcription for the word "Foglio". What does this word mean?

A. Pho-'yoh
B. Fo-gh-lioh
C. Fog-lioh

7) Find the correct transcription for the word "Uno". What does this word mean?

A. You-noh
B. Oo-noh
C. Uh-nh

8) Find the correct spelling for the word that sounds like "kohn-praa-reh". What does this word mean?

A. Comprare
B. Compurare
C. Comprarè

9) Find the correct spelling for the word that sounds like "ki-eh-deh-re".

A. Ciedere
B. Cedere
C. Chiedere

10) Find the correct spelling for the word that sounds like "ko-'nyo-me".

A. Coniome
B. Choniome
C. Cognome

Grammar exercises

11) Find the word that is not a masculine singular.

A. Gatto
B. Fatto
C. Amico
D. Mela

12) Find the word that is not a masculine plural.

A. Gnomi
B. Nomi
C. Uno
D. Zoo

13) Find the word that is not a feminine singular.

A. Uova
B. Porta
C. Bella
D. Amica

14) Find the word that is not a feminine plural.

A. Madri
B. Cane
C. Tasse
D. Ombre

15) Which of these words is not feminine?

A. Le prigioni

B. Le navi

C. Il mare

D. Le mele

16) Which of the following adj. + noun couples is correct?

   A. Gatto bella

   B. Fatto bello

   C. Amico belli

   D. Mela belle

17) Which of the following adj. + noun couples is correct?

   A. Tasse bella

   B. Prigioni belle

   C. Cane belle

   D. Madri belli

18) Which of the following adj. + noun couples is correct?

   A. Padri miei

   B. Tasse tuo

   C. Cane nostre

   D. Mela suo

19) Find the correct adjective for "chiesa".

   A. Mie

   B. Nostri

   C. Loro

   D. Essa

20) What word is compatible with the adj. "belle"?

   A. Padri

   B. Nostri

   C. Tasse

   D. Cane

21) How do you say "mine" in Italian?

A. Mio
B. Me
C. Mi
D. Io

22) How do you say "he" in Italian?

A. Esso
B. Lui/egli
C. Lei/ella
D. Gli

23) How do you say "their" in Italian?

A. Loro
B. Lui
C. Essi
D. Mio

24) How do you say "me" in Italian?

A. Me
B. Te
C. Mio
D. Io

25) What mood sets a condition?

A. Congiuntivo
B. Indicativo
C. Condizionale
D. Imperativo

26) What tense corresponds to the English future perfect?

A. Futuro anteriore
B. Imperfetto
C. Passato prossimo
D. Futuro semplice

27) Which of the following sentences is worded correctly?

  A. Una Marco ha mela.
  B. Marco ha una mela.
  C. Una ha mela marco.
  D. Mela ha una Marco.

28)   Which of the following sentences is worded correctly?

  A. Ha Marco mela.
  B. Ha una mela.
  C. Marco mela una.
  D. Ha Marco una.

29) Which of the following is a correct question?

  A. Marco ha una mela.
  B. Ha Marco una mela.
  C. Marco ha una mela?
  D. Marco una mela?

30)   Which of the following is a correct question?

  A. Marco ha una mela?
  B. Ha una mela marco?
  C. Ha Marco una mela?
  D. All of the above

ANSWERS		
1 → B, Apple	11 → D	21 → A
2 → C, Passport	12 → C	22 → B
3 → C, Car	13 → A	23 → A
4 → A, Church	14 → B	24 → A
5 → C, Gnome	15 → C	25 → C
6 → A, Sheet	16 → B	26 → A
7 → B, One or "a"	17 → B	27 → B
8 → A, To buy	18 → A	28 → B
9 → C	19 → C	29 → C
10 → C	20 → C	30 → D

PART ONE

TRAVELING IN ITALY

1.1
Introduction

Now that we have the basic knowledge to deal with whole sentences without too much trouble, we can start focusing on learning simple phrases and useful expressions. This first part will be about travel and the related vocabulary and expressions.

From this moment on, all the expressions will be provided together with the English translation or equivalent; if sometimes the wording of the English part sounds unusual or unnatural, it's because we're trying to formulate the sentence with a structure that is as similar as possible to the Italian one, to help you learn the correct and native-like Italian sentence structure.

Before we start, it might be useful to take a minute to talk about traveling in Italy, so that you know what the situation is like over there.

Italy is a rather small country and airports are mostly for international flights. Internal flights are rather expensive and oftentimes the wait at the airport can be longer than the flight itself. The majority of people move across the country by car or by train, which usually represents the best compromise between costs and comfort. Traveling by car can be quite costly, especially for long travels, because of two factors: the price of fuel, which is on average around 3 times higher than in the United States, and the cost of the highway, which can be up to ten euros per 100 kilometers (60 miles).

If you take the train, the cost of the ticket can be less than the cost of the highway alone. Buses are also an option, one of the cheapest, but usually not a very comfortable one, neither in terms of seats and luggage room, nor in terms of travel duration and frequency of the departures. If you trust people, car-pooling can be a very convenient option.

Ferry boats are not particularly costly, but they aren't inexpensive either. They might be the best option, depending on your destination and needs.

Taxis in Italy are not very common, with the only exceptions of Milan and Rome, and can be really expensive. As for the subways, only 7 cities in Italy offer some kind of underground-train transportation, and only in Milan the service is broad and efficient. Generally speaking, public transportation is more efficient in the north of the country than in the center-south.

Now that you know how things work, let's see what type of situations can occur to you, and when knowing Italian can help.

Long distances

When you need to travel long distances in Italy, it works pretty much in the same way with all the means of transport (train, airplane, bus and ferry). You can purchase the tickets online or at the station/airport/ dock, where there usually are both vending machines and ticket offices, with employees who speak English. In some cases (train, some bus companies, subway etc.) you're then asked to validate the ticket.

Most of these services are accessible for differently-abled people and people with difficulty of movement, but you might want to check with the company first; especially with trains, not all stations are equipped in the same way to respond to this and with some destinations it's better to notify the company, as they might need to get prepared. A simple example are stations where the platform is not at the same height as the train floor; all stations with this issue have specific equipment to lift wheelchairs on and off the train, and, if you notify them, they'll be waiting for you as the train arrives in the station.

Once you have the tickets, the next thing you have to do is find the place where you'll get on board. Let's take a look at a list of words that could help you in these passages; these words could be on your ticket or on the various signs you can see on the walls, posts and floors.

Travel Vocabulary			
Arrival(s)	l'arrivo/i	Mandatory to validate (the ticket)	Obbligo di convalida or Da convalidare
Baggage/Luggage	il bagaglio	Map	la mappa or la cartina
Boarding	l'imbarco	Mind the gap	Attenzione allo spazio tra treno e banchina
Booking/reservation	la prenotazione	No smoking	Vietato fumare
Cabin (ship)	la cabina	Platform	la banchina/ il binario
Car (train)	la carrozza	Police	la polizia
Cancellation	la cancellazione	Price/cost	il prezzo/ costo
Cancelled	cancellato	Rail	il binario

Checked baggage	il bagaglio in stiva	Seat	il posto (a sedere)
Changes	i cambi	Sightseeing	(il) Visitare
Class	la classe	Ticket	il biglietto
Customs	la dogana	Ticket office	la biglietteria
Delayed	In ritardo	Toll	il pedaggio/ casello
Departure(s)	la partenza/e	Vacation/holiday	la vacanza
Information desk	il punto/ centro informazioni	Valid for ... after validation	Valido per ... dopo la convalida
Journey	il viaggio	Valid until	Utilizzare entro il or Utilizzare dal ... al ...
Landing	l'atterraggio	To visit	Visitare
To leave	Partire	Welcome	Benvenuto

This table wants to collect in one place all the words that you might see around; in the next few chapters, we will give you the phonetic spelling as well when we're using the words for the first time.

Short distances

When traveling within a city or region, the best option could be renting a car, taking the train or taking a bus. Considering the efficiency of the various transports, traveling by bus is not often advisable; traveling by train only makes sense around cities, where there are numerous trains passing. In all the other cases, it is usually more convenient to rent a car or scooter.

Note that in some places, in Lombardy for example, you can buy a pass that is valid for any type of public transportation and lasts for a certain period (a day, a week, or a month). This is not the same thing as a city-pass, which is only valid for a single city and also includes discounts and free entry to some destinations.

TRAVELING BY BUS

Regional bus transportation works differently than inter-regional bus transportation, where you normally take a bus from, and to, a proper bus station. Local bus stops can be hard to spot, and are normally identifiable by 3 things:

- a yellow rectangle on the road with "bus" written on it; that's where the bus physically stops.
- a timetable. These can be in the form of a digital display, like in Milan, or a piece of paper on a post of some sort (usually green or orange), like in most countryside areas.
- a platform roof. In Italian it's called pensilina (*pen-see-lee-nah*), which specifically means a platform roof for waiting passengers.

In many cases, you cannot purchase the tickets on board. Sometimes you can buy them online, but not always. Tickets can be bought in train stations (buses always stop at train stations) or from local distributors, which are often places like newsstands or bodegas.

Always remember to validate the ticket once you're on board, there's an easy-to-find dedicated machine.

TRAVELING BY BIKE OR MOTORIZED SCOOTER

In many Italian cities, you can rent a bike or motorized stand-up scooter by simply subscribing to the service, for the period of time in which you are interested, and picking one up. Depending on the provider, there might be specific places to pick up and drop the bike/scooter, or you can leave it wherever you want within the city area, and find one through a GPS map. The service is brought to you through the apps of the various providers, and no human interaction is needed.

TRAVELING BY CAR

Traveling by car should not present many hindrances; there are only two points worth stressing:

- Italians are not the best drivers. Even though Italians can drive cars very well, at least on average, they're not very respectful of traffic laws. Especially in the south of the country, but actually pretty much everywhere, don't expect other drivers to always follow the laws, as it might be dangerous. It is not crazy land, but you might experience people cutting you off, or getting over your car... not in the safest way.
- Road signs can present short sentences in Italian, and it's clearly not possible to translate them on the go, you won't have time to do that. To help you with that, in the next paragraph we'll look into road signs vocabulary and some general advice.

ROAD SIGNS

Basic road signs are obviously easy to understand for most people, but there are a few types that can have words or phrases on them. One simple example is direction signs, but also signs like no-parking or no-entry can have specifications.

Here are some of the writings they can have on them:

- "Bollino blu". This writing, along with a lot of specifications, is frequently present under no-entry signs. You don't have to worry about that, it's about air pollution , and it only prohibits the passage of old vehicles with no antipollution systems.

- Time frames. Some signs indicate the time-frame within which the restriction is active. The writing might also say "on school days", "on the weekends" or something similar.
- "Eccetto…". Eccetto (*Eht-tchet-toh*) means "except" and it's usually under no-pass signs, specifying that vehicles like police vehicles or public-transport vehicles can pass.
- "Procedere a passo d'uomo" means "proceed at man speed", so cars need to drive very slowly.
- "Controllo elettronico della velocità" basically means "electronic speed check".

All these writings are on a white background; do not worry of writings on a different background color, as all mandatory indications are on white background.

Let's now take a look at this table, with the most common words you can find on direction signs. This includes the vocabulary for places related to transport.

Road-sign Vocabulary			
l'aeroporto	Airport	l'imbarco	Boarding (the dock)
la casa circondariale	Prison*	l'ospedale	Hospital
i carabinieri	Carabinieri**	il parcheggio	Parking
il centro sportivo	Sports center	i pedoni (e.g.. pedoni a destra or zona pedonale)	Pedestrians (e.g. pedestrians on the right or pedestrian zone)
il centro (storico)	(Old) city center	il porto	Harbor

la chiesa	Church	le poste, sometimes "Poste Italiane" or "Poste e telegrafo"	Post office
il cimitero	Cemetery	la stazione	Train station
la farmacia	Pharmacy	il veterinario	Veterinary
il municipio	Town hall	la zona industriale	Industrial area

* Prigione (*pree-djoh-neh*) is the most common word for prison, but on signs you'll find "casa circondariale"

** Carabinieri are basically also police; we'll talk about Italian police forces and emergency services later in the book.

Means of transport: vocabulary

We're now going to close this introduction with the last few words you need to know. Here are all the names for the most common means of transport:

Vehicle Vocabulary			
Bicycle	la bicicletta	Plane	l'aereo/aeroplano
Boat	la barca/nave	Ship	la nave
Bus	il bus/ l'autobus/ il pullman *	Scooter or Vespa	lo dcooter or il motorino
Car	l'auto/ automobile/ la macchina	Subway	la metro/ metropolitana
Carriage (with	la carrozza	Train	il treno

horses) or car (on a train)			
Ferry (Boat)	il traghetto	Tram	il tram** (*tr-raam*)
Motorcycle	la moto/ motocicletta	(by/on) Foot	(a) Piedi

* bus and autobus are pronounced like "*boos*" and "*ah-oo-toh-boos*". Pullman is "*Pool-maan*"

With the only exception of "a piedi", all other means of transport are preceded by the preposition "in":

To travel... = Viaggiare (*Vee-adj-djah-reh)*...

... by train = ...in treno (*een treh-noh*)
... by car = ...in macchina (*een muk-kee-nah*)
... by plane = ...in aereo (*een ah-eh-reh-oh*)

Take-home message

This introductory chapter was meant to give you some information that can help you when traveling in Italy. The linguistic portion of it will be further discussed in the rest of the book, and for now just focus on remembering the words that you think you need the most.

If you want more information to guide you in the aspects of traveling other than the language, you can check out our book:

"Italy Travel Guide: The Complete Guidebook to Plan Your Perfect Trip!"

1.2
Asking for information

Now we're getting into the thick of this book. From this moment on, we'll focus on the standard expressions you'll need to communicate with people who don't speak English, or with whom you're struggling to use English.

When you want to ask for information, you're most likely going to be speaking with strangers, for obvious reasons. For that reason, before we get to the expressions, it's time for us to introduce a new topic: the Italian polite form.

ITALIAN POLITE FORM

Italians have a peculiar way to express respect for the interlocutor, which they use when they're talking to a stranger (especially if older than you), to a senior, boss, parents in law, and other figures of authority. When it's people with whom you spend a lot of time, sometimes there's a mutual agreement on losing the polite form.

In Italian, the polite form is called "dare del Lei" (*daa-reh deh-l leh-ee* = call you a she), as opposite to "dare del tu" (*daa-reh deh-l too* = call you a you), and the name is pretty self-explanatory.

What happens is basically that, whenever you directly refer to the person, instead of using "you" (tu), you use "she" (Lei). This means that the pronouns will be in the feminine singular, and verbs will be in 3rd person singular. This happens regardless of the actual gender of the person. In writing, Lei, and the other pronouns for the person, are usually capitalized.

Let's see an example:

"Buongiorno, come sta (Lei)?" (*boo-ohn-djohr-noh, koh-meh stah?*)

This question in Italian can mean one of two things:

1. Good morning, how are you sir/madam?
2. Good morning, how is she?

From context, it's usually obvious which of the two it is.

"Lei" is usually omitted, as in Italian you can always omit the subject of a sentence when the subject is obvious. As we said, this question could be asked to either a man or a woman. Let's see when, on the contrary, gender does make a difference:

1. Lei è mai stato a Roma con Suo figlio? (*leh-ee èh maa-ee staht-oh ah Roh-mah kon soo-oh phee-'yoh?*)
2. Lei è mai stata a Roma con Suo figlio? (*leh-ee èh mah-ee staat-ah ah Roh-mah kon soo-oh phee-'yo?*)

This sentence means: "have you ever been in Rome with your son?"

The more perspicacious of you can probably already tell what's the gender of the two recipients of the question. The first question is asked to a man, the second to a woman; the difference is in stato/stata, and as usual the -o is for males and the -a for females.

This happens because, as we said, the pronouns are used in the feminine singular, and verbs are used in 3rd person singular. 3rd person and singular, but not necessarily feminine gender (unlike pronouns). Why is gender important if we're talking about verbs? Verbs don't have gender, they don't have an article or anything, right? Yes, that's usually true, but we mentioned participio passato, past participle. This tense can be used as a noun, to identify THE DOER of the action.

In Italian, composite verbs (in simple words, verbs that consist of two words) are made with participio passato, plus either the verb avere or essere (to have and to be). Because of this reason, all composite verbs innately have a gender, and when talking to a person you want to use the correct one. This can make it especially challenging to be gender-neutral when speaking Italian, but that's a different story.

On the other hand, there are situations in which it is usually common custom not to use the polite form, like when talking to a peer, colleague, or generic person with whom you have established an informal relationship. Sometimes elderly people tend not to use the polite form with younger people. Also, it is uncommon to use it with children.

Note that there are other ways to be polite in Italian, most of which are used similarly in English. An example is the use of the "condizionale" mood (which is similar to using "could you" instead of "can you" in English).

Now that you know how and when to be polite, let's get to the actual expressions.

Basic expressions to call for attention

When you want to start a conversation with someone you don't know, you usually have to say something like "excuse me" or "hello" to call for attention. In Italian, you do that just as well, and there are a few different ways depending on the circumstances.

If you want to talk to someone who expects that from you, like someone working at a desk (for example an agent at the info point, a cashier, an attendant, and so on), you probably want to use one of the following:

- Buongiorno (*boo-ohn-djohr-noh*) = Good morning
- Buonasera (*boo-ohn-ah seh-rah*) = Good evening
- Salve (*saal-veh*) = Hello (formal and polite)
- Ciao (*tchaaoh*) = Hello (informal, only with peers or younger people, and it might still sound rude)

The first three are pretty much interchangeable (Italians are often not precise with the use of good morning/evening, you can hear Buonasera starting mid-afternoon and Buongiorno basically all day long).

When you want to catch the attention of a passerby, or someone who's working but does not normally have to talk to people (police officer, trash collector, etc.), or someone who is simply not looking at you (e.g. a busy shop assistant), you can say:

- Mi scusi* (*mee scoo-see*) = excuse me (formal/ polite)
- Scusami (scusa me → scusami) (*scoo-sah-mee*) = excuse me (informal/peers and young interlocutors)

You can also combine the expressions, to say hello and call for attention, while excusing yourself for disturbing:

- Salve, mi scusi*, ... (*sahl-veh, mee scoo-see*) = Hello, sorry [for disturbing], (formal and polite)
- Ciao, scusami, ... (*tchaoh, scoo-sah-mee*) = Hello, sorry [for disturbing], (informal, only with peers or younger people)

* note that in Italian the same verb "scusarsi" is used both to say "excuse me" and "I'm sorry".

In both cases, the direct object (me) can be omitted, thus you can just say "scusi" or "scusa", as it is clear who is to be excused.

At the end of your question, you might want to add a "please". There are two main ways to say please in Italian:

- ...per favore (*per fah-voh-reh*) [common way]
- ...per cortesia (*per kor-teh-see-ah*) [alternative way]

Asking for information

Let's now see how to ask some simple questions in Italian (covering general situations, as the specific situations will be treated in detail in the specific sections):

[These questions can follow any of the introductory expressions seen above. Both the informal and polite form will be indicated when there is a difference.]

- **What's your name?**

Formal/Polite:

Come si chiama Lei? (*koh-meh see kee-ahm-ah leh-ee?*)

Informal:

Come ti chiami? (*koh-meh tee kee-ahm-ee?*) [Literally: how/what do you call yourself?]

- **Can you tell me...?** + (...what time it is; ...where's the toilet; ...if there's someone who speaks English)

Formal/Polite:

Mi sa dire...? (sa dire a me → mi sa dire) (*mee sah dee-reh...?*) [sa → verb sapere = to know/to know how to/to be able to]

Mi può dire...? (*mee poo-òh dee-reh...?*) [può → verb potere = to have the possibility to/to be able to]

Informal:

Mi sai dire...? (*mee sah-ee dee-reh...?*)

Mi puoi dire...? (*mee poo-oh-ee dee-reh...?*)

+

... che ore sono? (*keh oh-reh soh-noh?*) (what time is it?) [lit. what hours are they?]

... dov'è il bagno? (*dohv-èh eel bah-'nyoh?*) (where's the bathroom?) [dove è → dov'è]

... se c'è qualcuno che parla inglese? (*seh tch-èh kwahl-koo-noh keh par-lah een-gleh-seh?*) (...if there's someone who speaks english?) [ci è → c'è; "ci" is a pronominal particle meaning here or there]

- Are you waiting (in line)?

Siete in coda/fila? (*see-eh-teh een koh-dah/phee-lah?*) [lit. Are you (guys) (waiting) in line?]

Chi è l'ultimo? (*kee èh lool-tee-moh?*) [lit. Who is the last one (of the line)?]

Inizia qui la fila/coda? (*ee-nee-see-ah kwee lah phee-lah/koh-dah?*) [lit. Starts here line? = does the line start here?]

- Can you take a picture of us/of me?

Formal/Polite:

Ci/Mi può fare una foto? (*cee/mee poo-òh fah-reh oo-nah pho-toh?*) [to us = a noi → ci; to me = a me → mi]*

Informal:

Ci/Mi puoi fare una foto? (*cee/mee poo-oh-ee fah-reh oo-nah pho-toh?*) *

* in both the formal and informal form, the "ci" or "me" particle can merge with the verb and become "può farci/farmi una foto?" or "puoi farci/farmi una foto"? [farmi = *far-mee*; farci = *far-cee*]

- Do you mind if I...(smoke)?

SINGULAR:

Formal/Polite:

Le spiace se (fumo)? (*leh spee-ah-tcheh seh foo-moh?*) [spiace → verb spiacere = to mind/to be sorry]

Le dà fastidio se (fumo)? (*leh dah fahs-tee-dee-oh seh foo-moh?*) [dare fastidio = to bother/to give discomfort]

Informal:

Ti spiace se (fumo)? (*tee spee-ah-tcheh seh foo-moh?*)

Ti da fastidio se (fumo)? (*tee dah fahs-tee-dee-oh seh foo-moh?*)

PLURAL:

Vi spiace se (fumo)? (*vee spee-ah-tcheh seh foo-moh?*)

Vi da fastidio se (fumo)? (*vee dah fahs-tee-dee-oh seh foo-moh?*)

- Excuse me, <u>can you hold the dog</u>?

Formal/Polite:

Mi scusi, può tenere il cane? (*mee scoo-see, poo-òh teh-neh-reh eel kah-neh?*)

Informal:

Scusa, puoi tenere il cane? (*scoo-sah, poo-oh-ee teh-neh-reh eel kah-neh?*)

Excuse me, <u>are you...</u> (Mr. Rossi / a police officer)?

Formal/Polite:

Mi scusi, lei è... (il signor Rossi / un poliziotto)? (*mee scoo-see, leh-ee èh ... eel see-'nyor Ross-see / oon pol-ee-tzee-ot-toh ?*)

Informal:

Scusa, tu sei (Mario)? (*scoo-sah, too seh-ee Mah-ree-oh?*)

- Excuse me, <u>is this your ...</u> (phone; dog)?

Formal/Polite:

Mi scusi, è suo il... (telefono / cane)? (*mee scoo-see, èh soo-oh eel... teh-leh-foh-noh / kah-neh?*) [lit. excuse me, is the phone/dog yours?]

Informal:

Scusa, è tuo il (telefono / cane)? (*scoo-sah, èh too-oh eel... teh-leh-foh-noh / kah-neh?*)

- Excuse me, <u>can you help me</u>?

Formal/Polite:

Mi scusi, mi può aiutare? (*mee scoo-see, mee poo-òh ah-ee-oo-tah-reh?*)

also, "mi scusi, può aiutarmi?" (*ah-ee-oo-tahr-mee*)

Informal:

Scusa, mi puoi aiutare? (*scoo-sah, mee poo-oh-ee ah-ee-oo-tah-reh?*)

also, "scusa, puoi aiutarmi?" (*ah-ee-oo-tahr-mee*)

- <u>How old are you</u>?

Formal/Polite:

Quanti anni ha? (*kwaan-tee aan-nee ah?*) [lit. how many years does she (do you) have?]

Informal:

Quanti anni hai? (*kwaan-tee aan-nee ah-ee?*) [lit. how many years do you have?]

ASKING FOR DIRECTIONS

Asking for directions is one of the most likely scenarios for travelers of all kinds, even now that most people have smartphones. Let's see how to do that, keeping in mind that all of the following sentences can start off with a "mi scusi / scusa":

- <u>Where is</u>... (the Colosseum)?

Dov'è... (il Colosseo)? (*dohv-èh... eel Kohl-ohs-seh-oh*) [dove è → dov'è]

or

Sa/Sai dirmi dov'è (il Colosseo)? (*sah/sah-ee deer-mee dohv-èh... eel Kohl-ohs-seh-oh*) ["Sa" is in the polite form, "sai" is in the informal one]

66

- <u>Which way to</u>... Rome

Da che parte è... Roma? (*dah keh par-teh èh... Roh-mah?*) [lit. Which way is Rome?]

or

In che direzione è ... Roma? (*een keh deer-eh-zee-oh-neh èh... Roh-mah?*) [lit. In what direction is Rome?]

or

Dove devo andare per... Roma? (dohv-eh deh-voh ahn-dahr-eh per Roh-mah?) [lit. Where do I have to go for Rome?]

- <u>I'm looking for</u>... (the city center; Mr. Bianchi).

Sto cercando... (il centro storico; il signor Bianchi). (*stoh tcher-kahn-doh... eel tchen-troh stoh-ree-koh; eel see-'nyor Bee-ahn-kee*)

INTERNET CONNECTION

Nowadays, it almost sounds odd to talk about asking for information without mentioning the internet, so let's spend a word talking about the internet connection in Italy.

If you're planning to rely on free Wi-Fi, you should know that it is not available everywhere. Hotels, stations, and most restaurants offer a free Wi-Fi connection, but in other places like bars, cafeterias, gelaterie, and many other spots there is no available Wi-Fi. Also, usually, only customers are given the credentials to access the network, and the connection might be limited to certain websites.

On the other hand, prices for mobile connection are very low in Italy, which is why it usually makes the most sense to simply purchase a sim card from a local provider, to solve your connection issues. The average cost is between 10 and 30 euros a month for an unlimited data plan, and cheaper plans can cost as little as 5 euros for 30 days of service.

Take-home message

In this chapter you have met a lot of new expressions. Try to remember the ones you think you might need the most, and get familiar with the Italian phrasing, especially with questions.

More specifically, focus with extra effort on those expressions that are worded differently than English, and thus cannot be translated directly.

1.3
Tickets and timetables

When you travel, you necessarily have to deal with tickets and timetables. In this chapter, we'll go over the most common words and phrases related to this aspect of the journey.

Let's start with some vocabulary:

Ticket Vocabulary			
l'adulto	Adult	il numero	Number
gli anziani	Elderly	Obliterare (or Validare)	To validate (the ticket)
l'arrivo	Arrival	l'ora (la ora)	Time (lit. hour)
i bambini fino ai ... anni	Kids up to ... years old	l'orario (lo orario)	Timetable or Designated (arrival/departure) time
il biglietto	Ticket	l'ordinario	Standard (fee, ride etc.)
il cambio (treno)	(Train) change	la partenza	Departure
l'extraurbano	Suburban	il/i passeggero/i	Passenger/s
il feriale (Fer.)	on Weekdays	il prezzo	Price

il festivo (Fest.)	on Holidays	i ragazzi	Young adults (usually people between 12 and 18 y.o.)
la fermata	Stop	lo scalo	Stopover

In regard to timetables, you might find it useful to know the days of the week in Italian, and their abbreviations. Keep in mind that in Italy weeks start on Mondays:

L	M or Ma	M or Me	G	V	S	D
Lunedì	Marte-dì	Merco-ledì	Giove-dì	Vener-dì	Sabato	Dome-nica

Sometimes months might also be useful:

Gen	Feb	Mar	Apr	Mag	Giu
Gennaio	Febbraio	Marzo	Aprile	Maggio	Giugno
Lug	**Ago**	**Set**	**Ott**	**Nov**	**Dic**
Luglio	Agosto	Settemb-re	Ottobre	Novemb-re	Dicemb-re

Ok, now that we have covered the basic vocabulary, we can move on to the expressions and see how to use the words we just learned.

USEFUL EXPRESSIONS

As usual, keep in mind that you might want to introduce your sentence with either "buongiorno," or "mi scusi,", or with similar expressions.

- A ticket to/for Rome/the subway/two adults, please*.

Vorrei un biglietto per... (Roma/la metro/due adulti). [lit. I'd like (to buy) a ticket for...]

(*Vohr-reh-ee oon bee-'yet-toh per... Roh-mah/lah meh-troh/doo-eh ah-dool-tee*)

2/3/4 tickets (to Rome), please.

Vorrei due/tre/quattro... biglietti per (Roma).

(*Vohr-reh-ee doo-eh/treh/kwah-troh bee-'yet-tee per... Roh-mah*)

* In this case, the polite form is reached through the use of condizionale mood (vorrei) instead of indicativo (voglio) [verb volere = to want].

• What time does (the train/plane/ferry) to (Rome) leave/pass?

A che ora parte/passa...(il treno/l'aereo/il traghetto)... per... (Roma)?

(*Ah keh or-ah par-teh/pass-sah...eel treh-no/lah-eh-reh-oh/eel trah-get-toh... per Roh-mah?*)

[partire (parte) = to leave; passare (passa) = to pass/to pass by]

• Where does the (the train/plane/ferry) to (Rome) leave from?

Da dove parte...(il treno/l'aereo/il traghetto)... per... (Roma)?

(*Dah doh-veh par-teh... eel treh-no/lah-eh-reh-oh/eel trah-get-toh... per Roh-mah?*)

Alternatively:

Which...(platform/dock/gate/way) does the (train/ plane/ferry) to (Rome) leave from?

Da che... (binario/molo/gate/parte) parte il...(il treno/l'aereo/il traghetto)... per... (Roma)?

(Dah keh... bee-nah-ree-oh/moh-loh/gate/par-teh... par-teh eel treh-no/lah-eh-reh-oh/eel trah-get-toh... per Roh-mah?)

- How much is a ticket to Rome/for two adults?

Quanto costa un biglietto per...(Roma/due adulti)?

(Kwan-toh kos-tah oon bee-'yet-toh per... Roh-mah/doo-eh ah-dool-tee?)

How much are 2/3/4 tickets (to Rome/for an adult and a kid)?

Quanto costano due/tre/quattro biglietti per...(Roma/un adulto e un bambino)?

(Kwahn-toh kos-tah-noh doo-eh/treh/kwaht-troh bee-'yet-tee per... Roh-mah/oon ah-dool-toh eh oon bahm-bee-noh?)

- Where do they sell tickets for (the bus/the subway/the ferry boat)?

Dove vendono i biglietti per...(il bus/la metro/il traghetto)?

(Dov-eh ven-doh-noh ee bee-'yet-tee per... eel boos/lah met-roh/eel trah-get-toh?)

Where can I find the timetable for (the bus/the subway/the ferry boat)?

Dove posso trovare gli orari...(del bus/della metro/ del traghetto)?

(Dov-eh pos-soh troh-vah-reh 'yee oh-rah-ree... del boos/del-lah met-roh/del trah-get-toh?)

1.4
Renting a car

Our last chapter about traveling will focus on renting vehicles, typically cars, but also scooters, campers, boats and so on. The expressions stay the same.

If you have a chance to do so, renting a vehicle is probably the best way to experience Italy, because you can travel your own route and make the most out of the time you have available.

Note that most people in Italy drive cars with manual transmission, and most rented cars also have manual transmission (cambio manuale, *kaam-byo mahn-oo-ahl-eh*). If you want to rent a car with automatic transmission, you can ask if they have any:

"Avete (anche) macchine col cambio automatico?"

(Ah-veh-te (ahn-keh) maak-kee-neh kohl kaam-byo aoo-toh-mah-tee-koh)

Do you have (any) cars with automatic transmission?

Getting back to the lesson, let's quickly mention the Italian names for vehicles and items that are most commonly rented:

Renting Vocabulary			
Bike	la bicicletta/ bici	Motorboat	il motoscafo
Boat	la barca	Motorized scooter (stand-up scooter)	il monopattino elettrico
Camper	il camper (*kum-pher*)	Paddle boat	il pedalò
Car	l'auto(automobile)/ macchina	Quad bike/ATV	il quad (*kwohd*)
Climbing equipment	l'attrezzatu-ra da arrampicata	Scooter	lo scooter/ il motorino
Diving/snorkeling equipment	l'attrezzatura da sub (*soob*)/da snorkeling (*snor-keh-leeng*)	Skis	gli sci
Inflatable boat	il gommone	Sup	il sup (*Sup* or *Soop*)
Mobile home / trailer	la roulotte (*roo-lot*)	Surfboard	la tavola da surf (*surf*)
Motorbike	la moto	Yacht	lo yacht (*yot*)

Related Vocabulary			
Contract	il contratto	Keys	le chiavi
Distance	la distanza	Petrol	la benzina
Gasoline	il gasolio	Cost per day	il costo al giorno
Helmet	il casco	Cost per hour	il costo all'ora

Insurance	l'assicurazio-ne	Pump (fuel)	il distributore/ la Pompa di benzina
(driver's) License	la patente (di guida)	to Sign	Firmare
Jacket	la giacca	Trousers	i pantaloni

Ok, we've seen the words, let's now see how to use them!

USEFUL EXPRESSIONS

- I'd like to rent (a car/a scooter/a pair of skis).

Vorrei noleggiare*...(un'auto/uno scooter/degli sci).

(*Vohr-reh-ee noh-ledj-djar-eh... oon-aoo-toh/oo-noh scooter/deh-'yee shee*)

* Italians have 2 verbs for "to rent": noleggiare and affittare. Affittare works for everything, but is most common for things that you don't move, while noleggiare is for things you bring with you (car, skis, bike etc., but not a house, a hut, a parking spot, a beach spot with un umbrella etc.).

- How much is it to rent (a car/a scooter/a pair of skis)?

Quanto costa noleggiare...(un'auto/uno scooter/ degli sci)?

(*Kwan-toh kos-tah noh-ledj-djar-eh...oon-aoo-toh/oo-noh scooter/deh-'yee she?*)

- How much is it for the insurance?

Quanto costa l'assicurazione?

(*Kwan-toh kos-tah lahs-see-koo-rah-zee-oh-neh?*)

- Is it possible to rent (skiing/scuba diving/ climbing) equipment?

È possibile noleggiare l'attrezzatura da...(sci/sub/ arrampicata)?

(*Èh pos-see-bee-leh noh-ledj-djar-eh laht-trehz-zah-too-rah dah... she/ soob/ ar-rahm-pee-kaa-tah?*)

* <u>Can I rent</u> a (car/motorbike/camper) <u>with my driver's license</u>?

Posso noleggiare... (un'auto/una moto/un camper)... con la mia patente?

(*Pos-soh noh-ledj-djar-eh... oon-aoo-toh/oo-nah moh-toh/oon kum-per... kon lah mee-ah pah-ten-teh?*)

1.5
Let's practice!

This is our first session of practice with expressions. The following exercises will help you remember all that you have learned throughout these chapters, and give you a chance to practice pronunciation once again.

The exercises will be divided into three parts: in the first part we'll target vocabulary, in the second part we'll try and decipher Italian sentences about travel, and in the third part we'll do the opposite and try to say some sentences in Italian.

Vocabulary exercises

1) Match the word with the correct translation.

A	Treno
B	Partenze
C	Auto
D	Biglietto
E	Scalo
F	Arrivi

1	Stopover
2	Departures
3	Ticket
4	Luggage
5	Arrivals
6	Car

G	Bagagli			7	Train
H	Passaporto			8	Passport

2) Match the word with the correct translation.

A	Benzina			1	To help
B	Assicurazione			2	Timetable
C	Noleggiare			3	To buy
D	Orari			4	Car (train)
E	Comprare			5	To rent
F	Carrozza (train)			6	Platform
G	Binario (station)			7	Insurance
H	Aiutare			8	Petrol

3) Fill in the blanks.

I would like to buy a train ticket to Rome for two adults.

Vorrei ... un biglietto per ... per Roma per ....

    A. Noleggiare, treno, tre adulti
    B. Comprare, traino, due adulti
    C. Comprare, treno, due adulti

4) Fill in the blanks.

Hello kid, how old are you? What's your name?

... bambino, ... anni hai? Come ... ?

    A. Ciao, quanti, ti chiami
    B. Buongiorno, che, è il tuo nome
    C. Buongiorno, quanto, ti chiami

5) Fill in the blanks.

(to a police officer)

Excuse me, can you tell me where the Trevi Fountain is?

..., mi sa dire ... si trova la Fontana di Trevi?

    A. Scusa, come
    B. Scusami, dove
    C. Scusi, dove

Understanding Italian

In the following exercises, there will be a few sentences in Italian. After each paragraph, there will be a multiple choice, with a specific question or a choice between 3 different INTERPRETATIONS (not literal translation, as meaning is our focus) of the Italian sentences. Find the correct alternative.

Don't worry if there are words that you don't know, you're not supposed to precisely understand every word and sentence. The point is spotting the keywords that can drive our understanding process.

6) Ho comprato due biglietti del pullman per Roma e adesso sta per partire.

    A. I bought two tickets for the bus to Rome, and it's going to leave now.
    B. I bought two tickets for the ferry boat to Rome, and now it's about to arrive.
    C. I bought two tickets for the bus to Rome, and now it's about to arrive.

7) Buonasera, mi scusi, quanto costa questa giacca?

- Who are you most likely talking to? -

    A. A kid at the park

B. A travel agent

C. A shop assistant

8) Gli anziani con oltre 65 anni di età possono acquistare il
biglietto della metro a un prezzo ridotto.

A. People over 65 don't need a ticket to take the bus as it is
free.

B. The tram ticket costs less when the driver is older than 65.

C. People over 65 can purchase subway tickets at a reduced
price.

9) Il biglietto deve essere obliterato per essere ritenuto valido.

A. The ticket is valid for one flight.

B. The ticket must be kept on your person at any time.

C. Only validated tickets will be considered valid.

10) A: "Mi scusi, a che ora passa il treno per Napoli?"

B: "Dovrebbe passare alle 18:00, ma è in ritardo."

A. "A" is asking "B" where to take the train to Naples, "B"
replies that the train leaves from the main platform,
usually at 6PM.

B. "A" is asking "B" when the train to Naples will be leaving
the station, "B" replies that it should leave at 6PM, so "A"
should hurry up.

C. "A" is asking "B" when the train to Naples will arrive, "B"
replies that the train should pass by the station at 6PM,
but it's delayed.

Expressing yourself in Italian

In the following exercises, we'll try to say simple things in Italian.
You'll be given an English sentence or question, and you're asked
to choose the Italian alternative that best matches the original.
More than one answer may be correct.

11) Hello, can I have a ticket for two adults and a kid? She's six years old.

   A. Buongiorno, posso avere un biglietto per due adulti e una bambina? Ha sei anni.

   B. Salve, posso avere un pullman per due adulti e una bambina? È vecchia di sei anni.

   C. Buongiorno, posso avere un biglietto per due adulti e una chiesa? È vecchia di sei anni.

12) Excuse me, I wanted to know, can I take the train with my dog?

   A. Mi scusi, volevo sapere, posso pagare il gatto in treno?

   B. Mi scusi, volevo sapere, posso portare il cane in treno?

   C. Scusi, volevo sapere, posso portare il cane in treno?

13) Hello, how much is a first-class ticket to Bologna?

   A. Buongiorno, quanto porta un treno di prima classe per Bologna?

   B. Buongiorno, quanto costa un biglietto di prima classe per Bologna?

   C. Salve, quanto costa un biglietto di prima classe per Bologna?

14) Excuse me, does C54 [*random bus name in Italy*] pass from here? At what time?

   A. Scusami, il C54 passa di qui? A che ora?

   B. Mi scusi, il C54 passa di qui? A che ora?

   C. Scusami, il C54 passa di qui? A quale tempo?

15) There's a man who felt sick at platform 7, I already called 911.

   A. C'è un uomo che è stato male in piattaforma 7, io ho già chiamato il 911.

   B. C'è un uomo che è stato male alla piattaforma 7, ho già chiamato il 112.

C. C'è un uomo che è stato male al binario 7, ho già chiamato il 112.

16) Hello, little girl. Where are your parents?

    A. Ciao, piccolina. Dove sono i tuoi genitori?
    B. Ciao, piccolina. Quanto costano i tuoi parenti?
    C. Ciao, piccolina. Quanti sono i tuoi genitori?

ANSWERS	
1 → A7, B2, C6, D3, E1, F5, G4, H8	9 → C
	10 → C
2 → A8, B7, C5, D2, E3, F4, G6, H1	11 → A
	12 → B and C
3 → C	13 → B and C
4 → A	14 → A (formal/polite) and B (informal)
5 → C	
6 → A	15 → C
7 → C	16 → A
8 → C	

PART TWO

VISITING ITALY

2.1
Introduction

In this chapter, we'll continue our journey into the Italian language, but with a slightly different approach. At this point in the book, you are not an absolute beginner anymore, and thanks to that we can switch to a more dynamic approach.

From this moment on, the "lessons" will be more interactive. This chapter and the following one will be structured as follows: first, we'll take a look at the specific vocabulary related to the specific topic of the lesson; following, we'll go through the basic expressions that apply to the given scenario; last, we'll introduce secondary expressions in the form of practical exercises, which will have an explained solution coming right after the single exercise.

As always, at the end of each chapter there will be a practice session, with answers given only at the end of the session.

Before doing that, it might be helpful to summarize and schematize some of the expressions we have encountered so far, focusing on questions. The following table will compare English and Italian ways to ask some common questions.

The table will include phonetic transliteration, so take the chance to practice your pronunciation too.

Interrogative Pronouns			
How should I do this?	**Come** dovrei farlo? (*koh-meh dov-reh-ee far-loh?*) [fare quello → farlo]	What time is it?	Che ore sono? (*Keh oh-reh soh-noh?*) [lit. What hours are they?]
How do you say... in Italian?	Come si dice ... in Italiano?* (*koh-meh see dee-tche ... een ee-tah-leeah-noh?*)	**Where** is the Colosseum?	Dov'è il Colosseo? (*Dov-èh eel Kol-os-seh-oh?*) [Dove + e... = dov']
How old are you?	**Quanti anni** hai? (*Kwan-tee ahn-nee ahee?*) [lit. How many years do you have?]	Where can I buy tickets?	Dove posso comprare i biglietti? (*Dov-eh pos-soh kom-prah-reh ee bee-'yet-tee?*)
How much is it?	**Quanto** costa? (*Kwan-toh kos-tah?*) [lit. How much does it cost?]	**Which** wing of the museum should I visit first?	**Quale**** ala del museo dovrei visitare per prima? (*Kwal-eh al-ah del moo-seh-oh dov-reh-ee vee-see-tar-eh per pree-mah?*)
How many people live here?	**Quante** persone vivono qui? (*Kwan-teh per-soh-neh vee-voh-noh kwee?*)	From which platform does the train leave?	Da quale binario parte il treno? (*Dah kwal-eh bee-nah-reeoh par-teh eel treh-noh?*)

How long will this take?	Quanto ci vuole? (*Kwan-toh tchee voo-oh-leh?*)	Which is the fastest route?	Qual è la strada più veloce (tra queste)? (*Kwal-èh lah strah-dah peeòò veh-loh-tcheh?*)
When does the train leave?	Quando parte il treno? (Kwan-doh par-teh eel treh-noh?) or A che ora parte il treno? (*Ah keh orah par-teh eel treh-noh?*)	Who are you?	Chi sei tu? (*Kee seh-ee too?*)
When does it open?	Quando apre? (*Kwan-doh ah-preh?*)**	Who can I ask?	A chi posso chiedere? (*Ah kee pos-soh kee-ed-er-eh?*)
What can I buy tax-free?	Cosa*** posso comprare tax-free? (*Koh-sah pos-soh kom-prah-reh tax-free?*)	Why am I paying an extra cost?	Perché sto pagando un costo extra? (*Per-kéh stoh pah-gun-doh oon cost-oh extra?*)
What's that?	Cos'è quello? (*Kos-èh kwel-loh?*) [Cosa + vowel = cos']	Why? How come?	Perché? Come mai? (*Per-kéh? Kom-eh mahee?*)

* In this sentence, there is a particular type of structure called "si impersonale" (a "si" particle that makes the sentence "impersonal"). For the moment, just know that it exists and that it is used when the doer of the action is not specified.

** Remember that the specificity of verb conjugation in Italian lets you omit the subject and/or the direct object when they are not necessary.

*** In Italian, there is a word, "che" (*keh*), which can have several meanings. As a pronoun, it can be used for both "which" and "what", and in this second case it can both substitute "cosa" or couple it.

What's that? → Cos'è quello? OR Che è quello? OR Che cos'è quello?

From which platform? → Da quale binario? OR Da che binario?

Take-home message

In this chapter, we summarized and policed up some of the expressions that we have encountered so far. Since most of this lesson should not be new to you, you're asked to make an extra effort this time: try and remember all the expressions marked bold in the chapter.

2.2
Museums and sightseeing

We've already talked about how lessons are going to work from now on, so let's get to the vocab!

MUSEUM AND SIGHTSEEING VOCABULARY			
Audio guide/tour	l'audioguida	Guided tour	la visita guidata OR il percorso guidato*
Closing time	l'orario di chiusura	Opening time	l'orario di apertura
Clothing rules	il codice/ le regole di abbigliamento	Panoramic point / viewpoint	il punto panoramico
on Display	in mostra	Photos	le foto
Exhibit	la mostra	Prohibition	il divieto
Gallery	la galleria	Silence	il silenzio
Group rate/discount	lo sconto comitiva	Shop	il negozio
Guide (book and	la guida	Souvenir	il souvenir (soo-

person)			*veh-neer*)

* Visita guidata (*Vee-see-tah gooee-dah-tah*) is a guided tour with a physical guide, usually indoor. Percorso guidato (*Per-kor-soh gooee-dah-toh*) is a tour, usually outdoors, with no guide in person, but plaques with a description of the objects on display or historical sites.

After looking at the new vocabulary, it's time to use some of the words we just learned in our new expressions. Some of these expressions have parts in common with previously-encountered expressions, and the explanation of those parts will not be repeated. If there's something you don't remember, and you need to find that information again, you can take advantage of the quick handbook, where all previous and upcoming expressions are gathered.

USEFUL EXPRESSIONS

Explained:

- Where can I buy the city pass*?

Dove posso comprare il city pass?

(*Dov-eh pos-soh kom-prah-reh eel city paass?*)

*Many cities offer a city pass or city card that for a single price include a number of services or discounts, including public transportation, museum and tourist-attraction tickets, and discounts at some local shops.

- Are there discounts for... (students/kids/elderly)

Ci sono sconti per... (gli studenti/i bambini/gli anziani)?

(tchee *soh-noh skon-tee per... 'yee stoo-den-tee/ee bam-bee-nee/'yee ahn-tzeeah-nee?*)

- Can I take pictures of the objects on display? Can I take pictures with flash?

Si* possono fare foto degli oggetti in mostra? Si possono fare foto col flash?

(*See pos-soh-noh far-eh pho-toh de-'yee odj-djet-tee een mos-trah? See pos-soh-noh far-eh pho-toh kol flash?*)

* Another example of the use of "si impersonale", which is why there's a different wording than in English. This complex phrasing will not be further explained for the time being, just take it as it is and leave its grammar for your future studies. The next expression will also present this structure.

- Can I enter the church wearing shorts*?

Si può entrare in chiesa indossando i pantaloncini?

(*See poo-òh ent-rah-reh een kee-es-ah in-dos-sahn-doh ee pahn-ta-lon-cee-nee?*)

* In many churches and domes, people cannot enter when wearing clothes that are too informal or revealing, such as shorts, short skirts, and low-cut or sleeveless tops. This is for both men and women.

Interactive learning:

In the next part, you'll be given an English expression and 3 possible alternatives for the Italian equivalent. You'll have to guess which is the correct one and, if you guessed wrong, the answer below will show you the mental process you could have followed.

- What time does the museum open/close?
    1. Che ora apre/chiude il museo?
    2. A che ora apre/chiude il museo?
    3. Che tempo apre/chiude il museo?

Answer:

The correct alternative is the second one. You can rule out number 3 because we've seen multiple times that "time" is translated with "ora" when it's about timetables and clocks. Both number 1 and 2 would be fair guesses, but in Italian the preposition "a" is needed for that complement.

(*Ah keh orah ap-reh/keeoo-deh eel moo-seh-oh?*)

- Is it possible to have an English guide / audio guide / guidebook?

    1. È possibile avere una guida/audioguida in inglese?
    2. È possibile di avere una guida/audioguida in inglese?
    3. È possibile avrò una guida/audioguida in inglese?

Answer:

You can rule out number 3 because you need an infinitive, and that's not the infinitive for verb avere (that's simple future 1st per. sin.). It's a harder call between number 1 and 2, but no preposition is needed here as the verb avere is the subject of the sentence.

Note that the italian word "guida" translates both a person who's a guide and a guidebook.

(*Èh pos-see-bee-leh ah-veh-reh oonah gooee-dah/ah-oo-deeoh gooee-dah een een-gleh-seh?*)

- How long does the tour take?

    1. Come dura la visita?
    2. Quanto lungo è la visita?
    3. Quanto dura la visita?

Answer:

The correct alternative is the last one. We can rule out number one because we've seen before that "how long" translates to "quanto + a word for time". Number 2 might have been correct-ish, but the noun and adjective do not agree in gender.

(*Kwan-toh doo-rah lah vee-see-tah?*)

2.3
Exploring nature: mountains, sea and countryside

You know the drill: first the vocabulary, then the expressions. In these chapters, try to focus on the constructions that we have already seen before; if you see them often, it's because they're very common.

VOCABULARY

Mountain Vocabulary			
Backpack	lo zaino	Mountain hut	il rifugio
Bonfire	il falò or il fuoco da campo	Ski resort	l'impianto sciistico
Cable Car	la funivia	Track	il sentiero
Hike	l'escursione	Trekking guide	la guida ai sentieri

Sea and Beach Vocabulary			
Beach	la spiaggia	Sunbathing	prendere il sole
Beach umbrella	l'ombrellone	Sunscreen	la crema solare
Fishing	la pesca or pescare*	Swim	Nuotare or Fare il bagno**
Beach lounger/chair	il lettino (da spiaggia)	Swimsuit	il costume da bagno

* Pescare (*Pes-kah-reh*) is the action of fishing. Pesca (*Pes-kah*) is the name of the sport/hobby.

** Nuotare (Noo-oh-tah-reh) is the action of swimming, and you can nuotare at sea, at the lake, or in a pool. Fare il bagno is the action of relaxing in the water, and it's unusual to use it for swimming pools, especially if they have lanes. Fare il bagno also means to take a bath in a bathtub or similar.

Countryside Vocabulary			
Agritourism / Holiday Farm	l'agriturismo	SPA / Thermal baths	la SPA / le terme
Camping	il campeggio	Tasting (food and wine)	la degustazione
Horse ride	il giro/ la gita a cavallo	Trip	la gita
Lake	il lago	Winery	l'azienda vinicola

EXPRESSIONS

This time there will only be interactive learning. You'll be given an English expression and 3 possible alternatives. Choose wisely, my young padawan, and practice pronunciation with the transliterated answers.

- The ski resort is open from November 1st to March 31st. During the rest of the year, you can still enjoy our landscapes, tracks, and food (at the mountain hut).

- Find the equivalent -

1. L'impianto sciistico è chiuso da Novembre 1 a Marzo 31. Durante il resto dell'anno, puoi sempre goderti i nostri panorami, i nostri sentieri e il nostro bibo (al rifugio).
2. L'impianto sciistico è chiuso dall'1/11 al 31/3. Durante il resto dell'anno, puoi sempre goderti i nostri panorami, i nostri sentieri e il nostro cibo (al rifugio).
3. L'impianto sciistico è aperto dall'1/11 al 31/3. Durante il resto dell'anno, puoi sempre goderti i nostri panorami, i nostri sentieri e il nostro bibo (al rifugio).

Answer:

If you remember what aperto and chiuso mean, it was probably easy for you to tell that the correct answer was number 3. In case you didn't know, note that in Italy dates are always DD/MM/YY and not MM/DD/YY.

(*Leem-pee-an-toh she-eest-ee-koh èh keeoo-soh dahl-loon-oh oon-dee-tchee al tren-too-noh treh. Doo-ran-teh eel rest-oh del-lan-noh, poo-oh-ee sem-preh go-der-tee ee nos-tree pan-or-am-ee, ee nost-tree sen-tee-er-ee eh eel nos-troh cee-boh (al ree-foo-geeoh)*))

- I would like to <u>rent a beach umbrella</u> and two beach loungers, please.

- Find the equivalent -

1. Vorrei affittare un ombrello da spiaggia e due lettini, per favore.
2. Vorrei affittare un ombrellone e due lettini, per favore.

3. Vorrei noleggiare un ombrellone e due lettini, per favore.

Answer:

You can rule out number one because we've just seen that the Italian for beach umbrella is "ombrellone" (= big umbrella). Number 2 and 3 are both theoretically correct, but usually you cannot move the umbrella and chairs you rent, so number 2 is more correct. If you don't remember why, go back to the "renting a car" chapter for the difference between affittare and noleggiare.

(*Vor-reh-ee nol-edj-djar-eh oon om-brehl-loh-neh eh doo-eh let-tee-nee, per pha-vor-eh.*)

- Fill in the following sentences using A or B.

A: fare il bagno

B: nuotare.

1. Il sole è troppo caldo, vado a … .
1. (The sun is too hot, I'll go …)
2. Stavo … in piscina quando dei bambini hanno invaso la mia corsia.
2. (I was … in the pool when some kids invaded my lane.)
3. Marco ha preso il suo delfino gonfiabile ed è andato in acqua a … .
3. (Marco took his inflatable dolphin and went in the water to …)

Answer:

Both A and B work for number one, the person could both relax or go for a proper swim. B is the correct answer for number 2, as, in pools that have lanes, you don't usually just dip yourself in. The answer to number 3 is A, as not many Olympic swimmers compete while riding inflatable toys.

- Tomorrow we'll go to a holiday farm for a horse ride and a wine and prosciutto tasting. Did I bring my mosquito repellent?

- Find the equivalent -

1. Oggi andiamo in un agriturismo per fare un giro a cavallo e una degustazione di vini e prosciutto. Ho preso lo spray antizanzare?
2. Domani andremo in un agriturismo per fare un giro a cavallo e una degustazione di vini e prosciutto. Ho preso lo spray antizanzare?
3. Ieri siamo andati in un agriturismo per fare un giro a cavallo e una degustazione di vini e prosciutto. Ho preso lo spray antizanzare?

Answer:

The correct answer is number 2. Oggi is today, domani is tomorrow, ieri is yesterday. Also, the verbs are in the present, future, and past tense.

(*Doh-mah-nee an-dreh-moh een oon ah-gree-too-ree-smoh per fah-reh oon gee-roh ah cah-val-loh eh oona de-goos-tah-zeeoh-neh dee vee-nee eh pro-she-oot-toh. Oh pre-soh lo spraay aan-tee-zaan-zaa-reh?*)

2.4
Restaurants and Food

Here is some useful vocabulary about restaurants, drinking and food:

Restaurant and Bar Vocabulary			
Bar (pub, club)	il bar (il pub, la discoteca)	Plate	il piatto
Barman	il barman/ il barista	Receipt	lo scontrino
to Book	Prenotare	Restaurant	il ristorante
Beers	la birra in bottiglia birra piccola (10 oz) birra media (14 oz) pinta di birra (17 oz) birra da litro (34 oz)	Salt	il sale
Bill	il conto	Shaken, not stirred	Agitato, non mescolato

Chopsticks	le bacchette (cinesi)	Split the bill	Dividere il conto
Drink	il drink	Spoon	il cucchiaio
Fork	la forchetta	Stake (blue, red, medium red, medium, medium well, well done)	la bistecca or la costata: blue, al sangue, media / al sangue, media cottura, media / ben cotta, ben cotta
Leftovers	gli avanzi	Table	il tavolo
Knife	il coltello	Take-out	l'asporto, or il take-away, or la consegna a domicilio
Gelateria	la gelateria	Tip	la mancia
Glass (a glass)	il bicchiere	Toilet	La toilette (*twaa-let*), or il bagno, or i servizi
Pizzeria	la pizzeria	Waiter/waitress	il cameriere/ la cameriera
Parmesan	il parmigiano / il formaggio grattugiato	Water (tap, bottled, uncarbonated, carbonated)	l'acqua: del rubinetto, in bottiglia, naturale, gassata o frizzante
Pepper	il pepe	Wine (red, white, pink)	il vino: rosso, rosa, rosé

USEFUL EXPRESSIONS

Explained expressions

- <u>I'm allergic/intolerant</u> to... (gluten, strawberries)

Sono allergico/intollerante... (al glutine, alle fragole)

(*Soh-noh al-ler-djee-koh/een-tol-leh-rahn-teh...al gloo-tee-neh, al-leh fra-go-leh*)

- Can <u>people with disabilities</u> access your building?

Le persone disabili riescono* ad accedere al vostro edificio?

(*Leh per-soh-neh dees-ah-bee-lee ree-es-koh-noh ahd atch-tche-deh-reh al vos-troh eh-dee-fee-tcho?*)

* When you want to use "can/be able to" in Italian, you have a few specific alternatives. The predominant ones are potere and riuscire. The former means to be able in terms of potentiality. The latter means to actually be able to succeed.

Interactive learning

Choose the best equivalent for the given Italian expressions about food and restaurants. Take the chance to practice your pronunciation as well.

- Buonasera, vorrei prenotare un tavolo per quattro persone per le 21.

   1. Good evening, I would like to have a table for four people over 21.
   2. Good evening, I would like to book a table for four people at 9 PM.
   3. Good evening, I would like to book a table for four people over 21.

Answer:

The truth lies in the middle.

(Boo-oh-nah seh-rah, vor-reh-ee preh-no-tah-reh oon tah-voh-loh per kwat-troh per-soh-neh per leh vent-oo-noh)

- Buongiorno, vorrei ordinare una pizza con consegna a domicilio.

    1. Hello, I would like to order a pizza with delivery.
    2. Hello, I would like to order a pizza with consequences on the dome.
    3. Hello, I would like to order a take-out pizza.

Answer:

If you think it's number 2, get back to page 1 and start this book all over again. If you guessed either 1 or 3, good job. The best alternative is number one, because consegna a domicilio literally means "home delivery", while take-out might suggest that you are going to bring it home yourself.

(Boo-ohn-djohr-noh, vor-reh-ee or-dee-nah-reh oonah pitz-tza kon kon-seh-'nee-ah ah doh-mee-tchee-lee-oh.)

- Mi scusi, è possibile portare a casa gli avanzi?

    1. Excuse me, is it possible to take home the chopsticks?
    2. Excuse me, is it possible to take the waiter home?
    3. Excuse me, is it possible to take home the leftovers?

Answer:

I'm sorry, the answer is not number 2. It's number 3. This was mere vocabulary, so no explanation should feel needed.

(Mee scoo-see èh pos-see-bee-leh por-tah-reh ah cah-sah 'yee ah-vaan-tzee?)

- A: "È vero che in Italia è prassi non lasciare la mancia al cameriere?"
  B: "Sì, ma i camerieri non si arrabbiano di certo se lo fai."

1. A: "Is it true that in Italy it is standard practice not to tip the waiter?"
   B: "Yes, but waiters surely don't get mad if you do."

2. A: "Is it true that in Italy it is standard practice not to tip the waiter?"
   B: "Yes, but waiters don't usually get mad if you do."

3. A: "Is it true that in Italy it is not standard practice to tip the waiter?"
   B: "Yes, but waiters don't usually get mad if you do."

Answer:

The first one is correct. The only difference from the others is in the reply sentence, where "di certo" means "certainly, for sure".

(*A: "Èh veh-roh keh een ee-taa-leeah èh pras-see non lah-shaa-reh lah maan-tchah al kah-meh-ree-eh-reh?"*

B: "See, mah ee kah-meh-ree-eh-ree non see ar-raab-bee-ah-noh dee tcher-toh deh loh pha-ee.")

2.5
Churches and places of worship

Italy is a secular state and, even though there is a vast predominance of Catholics, all religions are welcome. Around Italian cities you can find churches, mosques, temples, synagogues, and other places of worship, but far from big cities it is rare to find other churches than Catholic churches, unfortunately.

Let's quickly go over some vocabulary, and then we'll see a couple of expressions.

Religion Vocabulary			
Chapel	la cappella	Mosque	la moschea
Cathedral	la cattedrale	Pilgrimage	il pellegrinaggio
Church	la chiesa	Prayer	la preghiera
Cemetery	il cimitero	Stations of the cross	la Via crucis
Dome	il duomo	Synagogue	la sinagoga
Mass	la messa	Temple	il tempio

Italy is also a destination to thousands of believers who every year travel to Rome in pilgrimage; because of this, the country is ready to meet the need of religious people of all denominations, but Christians, and Catholics specifically, will definitely have an easy life.

USEFUL EXPRESSIONS

The expressions related with this topic do not have anything particular that we haven't already encountered, so it's just a matter of using the new words in the phrases we have seen in the previous chapters.

We'll just make a couple of quick examples in the form of a multiple choice exercise, like we have done before.

- A che ora inizia la messa? In che giorni c'è la messa?

    1. What time does mass start? On what days is there mass?
    2. Does mass last one hour? On which days does it?
    3. Will mass begin in an hour? On which days does it happen?

Answer:

The first is correct. As we have seen before, that's the Italian formulation for asking about the time.

(*Ah keh or-ah ee-nee-tzeeah lah mes-sah? Een keh djor-nee chèh lah mes-sah?*)

- Mi scusi, dove si trova la chiesa del paese?

    1. Excuse me, where is the church of the country?
    2. Excuse me, where is the church of this town/ village?
    3. Excuse me, when was this church built?

Answer:

The last one is clearly incorrect. The first and second are both linguistically correct, as paese means both village and country, but in this second case the sentence wouldn't make much sense. So, number two is correct.

(*Mee skoo-see, dov-eh see troh-vah lah kee-eh-sah del pah-eh-seh?*)

106

2.6
On the telephone

In this chapter, we'll see how a phone call works in Italian; we'll mention the basic mechanism, starting from common expressions.

In this case, there's not much vocabulary involved, at least not vocabulary that you would likely need. What we are going to do instead is compare the expressions used when talking on the phone.

EN	IT
Hello? [picking up the phone]	Pronto?*
Hello? Who is this?	Pronto? Chi parla?
Hello? Can you hear me? [unstable signal]	Pronto? Mi senti? [informal] or Pronto? Mi sente? [polite]
Hi, it's John, do you have a minute?	Ciao, sono** Giovanni, hai un attimo / un minuto?
You can call me back at 123-456-789	Puoi richiamarmi all'123-456-789 [inf.] Può richiamarmi all'123-456-789 [polite]
Call me back when you can	Richiamami quando puoi/riesci

Ok, thank you, bye!	Ok, la ringrazio, a risentirci***! [polite] Ok, grazie, ciao!**** [informal]

* When Italians pick up the phone, the first thing they say is always "pronto", usually with an interrogative tone (pronto?). It translates the English "hello", but literally it means "ready", or, more commonly, "ready?".

** On the phone, in English we say "Hi, it's me", but in Italian it is "Hi, I'm me" → "Ciao, sono io".

*** Italians are often long-winded when hanging up, so you might hear a call ending with "la ringrazio, salve, arrivederci, buona giornata" or a different series of expressions. "A risentirci" (*ah ree-sen-teer-tche*) means "until we hear again from each other".

**** When it's an informal situation, Italians get even more long-winded and you can hear friends ending a call with "ok, dai, ci sentiamo, sì, ciao, ciao, cia, cia ,cia, ciao" or a similar ramble.

2.7
Seeking help or assistance

This lesson and the next one will be mostly focused on the expressions per se, rather than the language and the structures. Considering the topic, it's best to focus on clarity and precision of the message rather than understanding the sentence structure.

Before doing that, let's quickly explain what it means to have an emergency in Italy. If you have a medical emergency, it is pretty simple: you call 112, an ambulance from any provider comes and picks you up, and it brings you to the nearest hospital. Transport and first-aid treatments are always free for everybody, as long as there is evidence of the urgency.

If you have a different type of emergency, what happens depends on the emergency. You can call 112 for any type of situation, but different forces will respond to the call depending on the case.

In Italy, there are different police forces, the main of which are 4: Polizia, Carabinieri, Guardia di Finanza and Polizia Locale. Polizia and Carabinieri basically do the same things that the police do in America, with the difference that Carabinieri are technically part of the army. Polizia Locale are traffic police. Guardia di Finanza mostly works with tax evasion and the black markets (typically drugs). All these agencies coexist under the same jurisdictions, so any of these could respond to the call, depending on the situation.

That's all for our introduction, so let's get back to the language and start looking at some vocabulary:

Emergency Vocabulary			
911	il 112	Officer	l'agente
Ambulance	l'ambulanza	Police	la polizia
Bomb	la bomba	Red Cross	la Croce Rossa
Doctor	il dottore or il medico	Rescue team	la squadra di soccorso
Fire	l'incendio	Shoots	gli spari
Help!	Aiuto!	SOS	il/l' SOS (sohs or es-seh oh es-seh)

Now that we know what words are coming, we can start looking at the expressions. We will group them up in a table, next to their translation and transliteration (for pronunciation).

IT	EN	Transliteration
Mi scusi, mi può aiutare?	Excuse me, can you help me? [polite]	*Mee scoo-see, mee poo-òh ah-eeoo-tah-reh?*
Scusa, mi puoi aiutare?	Excuse me, can you help me? [informal]	*Scoo-sah, mee poo-òh ah-eeoo-tah-reh?*
Ho un problema alla macchina.	I have an issue with my car.	*Oh oon proh-bleh-mah al-lah maak-kee-nah*
Ho perso il portafogli / il cellulare.	I lost my wallet / phone.	*Oh per-soh eel por-tah-pho-'yee / eel tchel-loo-lah-reh.*
Ho sentito degli spari!	I heard gunshots!	*Oh sen-tee-toh de-'yee spa-ree!*

C'è un allarme bomba nella metro.	Theres a bomb alert in the subway.	*Tchè oon al-lar-meh bom-bah nel-lah met-roh.*
Ho bisogno di un'ambulanza.	I need an ambulance.	*Oh bee-so-'nyo dee oon am-boo-lahn-tzah*
C'è una donna che si è sentita male, chiamate il 112.	There's a woman who felt sick, call 911.	*Tchè oon-ah don-nah keh see èh sen-tee-tah maa-leh, keeaa-maa-teh eel tchen-toh-doh-dee-tchee.*
Scusa, mi puoi dare una mano?	Sorry, can you give me a hand? [informal]	*Scoo-sah mee poo-oh-ee daa-reh oo-nah maa-noh?*
Non trovo più mia figlia, mi può aiutare?	I can't find my daughter, can you help me?	*Non troh-voh pee-òò meeah phee-'yah, mee poo-òh aa-eeoo-taa-reh?*

2.8
Hospital, ER, Police

Now that we have seen the basic expression to call for help, let's analyze the various situations more in depth. It's time for a second round of vocabulary:

Emergency Vocabulary 2			
Accident	l'incidente	Hospital	l'ospedale
to Arrest	Arrestare	to feel it Hurt	Fare male
Broken	Rotto	Injured	Ferito
Drunk	Ubriaco	Severe	Grave
ER	PS (Pronto Soccorso)	Stolen	Rubato
Fireman	Vigile del Fuoco	Surgery	l'operazione chirurgica

Like in the previous chapter, we will now focus on the expressions, presented to you in the form of a table:

IT	EN	Transliteration
Dove si trova il Pronto Soccorso?	Where's the ER?	*Doh-veh see troh-vah eel pron.toh sok-kor-soh?*
Come sta (mio marito)?	How's (my husband)?	*Kom-eh stàh (meeoh maa-ree-toh?)*
È grave? Mi dovrei preoccupare?	Is it bad? Should I be worried?	*Èh graa.veh? Mee dov-reh-ee preh-ok-koo-paa-reh?*
Mi fa male il braccio.	My arm hurts.	*Mee pha maa-leh eel braatch-tcho.*
Credo di avere una gamba rotta.	I think I have a broken leg.	*Kreh-doh dee aa-veh-reh oo-nah gaam-bah rot-tah.*
Mi sento svenire.	I feel like fainting.	*Mee sen-toh sveh-nee-reh.*
Ho la nausea. Mi viene da vomitare.	I have nausea. I feel like vomiting.	*Oh lah now-seh-ah. Mee vee-eh-neh daa voh-mee-taa-reh.*
Sento un dolore al petto.	I feel a pain in my chest.	*Sen-toh oon doh-loh-reh nehl pet-toh.*
Mi hanno rubato la borsa / il cellulare.	They stole my bag / my phone.	*Mee an-noh roo-baa-toh lah bor-sah / eel tchel-loo-laa-reh.*
Hanno rapito mio figlio!	They kidnapped my son!	*An-noh raa-pee-toh meeoh phee-'yoh!*

2.9
Let's practice!

You have completed the third part of this book, the second concerning expressions. Are you happy? Do you feel like you understand Italian better now? I really hope so.

Considering that this part consisted of large portions of practice and exercises, this practice session will be broader than part one's, so that we won't simply repeat the exercises we encountered in the various chapters of this second part of the book.

Following, you will find twenty exercises that randomly target the topics discussed in this part two. This does not mean that the information learned in part one and zero will not be needed; we want to keep practicing and be able to rely on every brick we have laid.

A little tip before we start: remember that in Italian articles and adjectives have to agree in gender and number with the nouns. This can help you choose the correct word when there's a matter of gender or number. This also means that it's common to see clusters of words all ending in the same vowel: O, A, I or E.

EXERCISES:

1) Fill in the blanks:

Per entrare al museo devo comprare il ..., ma non vedo la ....

   A. passaporto, commessa
   B. biglietto, biglietteria
   C. carta, cartoleria

2) Fill in the blanks:

... devo andare a una degustazione di vini in un ... in ....

   A. oggi, agriturismo, campagna
   B. oggi, ospedale, città
   C. guida, cane, centro

3) Fill in the blanks:

Vorrei ... un tavolo per domani sera alle ..., per favore non vicino al ...

   A. prenotare, 21, bagno
   B. comprare, 18, centro
   C. prenotare, 12, bagno

4) Fill in the blanks:

...? Chi parla? ..., non la sento bene al telefono, può ...?

   A. ciao, aiuto, pagare
   B. pronto, scusami, chiamarmi
   C. pronto, mi scusi, richiamarmi

5) Fill in the blanks:

Posso portare il ... nel ...?

   A. patente, automobile
   B. cane, ristorante
   C. soldi, comprare

6) Fill in the blanks:

Mia ... ha 6 anni. Il biglietto ha un ... ridotto?

   A. figlio, biglietteria

B. figlia, costo

C. figlio, pagare

7) Fill in the blanks:

... una birra media chiara, ...:

A. posso, piacere
B. portare, pinta
C. vorrei, per favore

8) Find the best English equivalent (more than one answer may be right):

Voglio noleggiare uno scooter per andare a fare una gita intorno al lago.

A. I want to rent a scooter to go out on a trip around the lake.
B. I want to buy a scooter to go rock-climbing near the lake.
C. I want to rent a scooter to enjoy my stay at the lake.

9) Find the best English equivalent (more than one answer may be right):

A: Mi scusi, lei è italiano?
B: No, sono americano.

A. A: Excuse me, do you speak Italian?
   B: No, I speak American English.

B. A: Excuse me, are you Italian?
   B: No, I'm American.

C. A: Excuse me, is she Italian?

D. B: No, she's American.

10) Find the best English equivalent (more than one answer may be right):

I biglietti costano cinque euro a persona.

A. The ticket costs six euros per person.
B. The tickets cost five euros per person.

C. The ticket costs five euros per person.

11) Find the best English equivalent (more than one answer may be right):

Dove si trova il negozio di souvenir?

    A. Where's the souvenir shop?
    B. How much is this souvenir?
    C. Where's this souvenir from?

12) Find the best English equivalent (more than one answer may be right):

Quanti anni ha? Da dove viene?

    A. How old are you? Where are you from?
    B. How many years does it have? How much is it?
    C. How old is she? Where is she from?

13) Find the best English equivalent (more than one answer may be right):

È possibile avere una guida che ci possa parlare degli oggetti in mostra?

    A. Is it possible to have a guide who can tell us about the objects on display?
    B. Is it possible to have a guidebook that can tell us about the objects on display?
    C. Is it possible to have an audio guide that can tell us about the objects on display?

14) Find the best English equivalent (more than one answer may be right):

Il museo chiude alle 20.00.

    A. The museum opens at 8 AM.
    B. The museum closes at 2 AM.
    C. The museum closes at 8 PM.

15) Find the best Italian equivalent (more than one answer may be right):

How much is it to visit the Colosseum?

    A. Quanto costa visitare il Colosseo?
    B. Quanto ci vuole per visitare il Colosseo?
    C. Come costa visitare il Colosseo?

16) Find the best Italian equivalent (more than one answer may be right):

How long does it take to go to Rome?

    A. Quanto è lungo per arrivare a Roma?
    B. Quanto ci vuole per arrivare a Roma?
    C. Quanto ci vuole per andare a Roma?

17) Find the best Italian equivalent (more than one answer may be right):

A: Do you speak Italian?
B: Yes, but just a little bit.

    A. A: Sei italiano?
       B: Sì, ma solo per metà.

    B. A: Parli italiano?
       B: Sì, ma solo un pochino.

    C. A: Parli italiano?
    D. B: Sì, sono un maestro ora.

18) Find the best Italian equivalent (more than one answer may be right):

How much are those apples?

    A. Quante sono quelle mele?
    B. Quanto costano quelle mele?
    C. Come costano quelle mele?

19) Find the best Italian equivalent (more than one answer may be right):

I lost my dog, did you see a black Labrador?

    A. Ho perso il mio cane, ha visto un labrador nero?
    B. Ho perso il mio cane, hai visto un labrador nero?
    C. Non trovo più il mio cane, ha visto un labrador nero?

20) Find the best Italian equivalent (more than one answer may be right):

Where can I find the timetable for the masses?

    A. Dove posso prendere i tavoli del tempo per le messe?
    B. Dove posso fondere le ore per la messa?
    C. Dove posso trovare gli orari delle messe?

ANSWERS	
1 → B	11 → A
2 → A	12 → A and C
3 → A	13 → A and B
4 → C	14 → C
5 → B	15 → A
6 → B	16 → C is the best matching
7 → C	one, but B is also correct
8 → A	17 → B
9 → B	18 → B
10 → B	19 → A, B and C
	20 → C

PART THREE

LIVING ITALY

3.1
Introduction

We are now starting a new part of the book, the third and last group of our thematic lessons. With this new group, we are going to continue with the same approach that we have adopted for part two, with less explaining and more interactive learning.

The goal is not to avoid mistakes, but learn from them. Focus on understanding your mistakes, and you'll speed up your learning process like petrol on a bonfire.

Before we skip to the good part, let's take advantage of this introductory chapter and lesson to introduce you to a new topic: answering questions.

ANSWERING QUESTIONS

So far, we have been focused on asking questions and obtaining information, but we've been giving very little space to answering questions and giving information. It's time for us to investigate this topic as well.

Let's start by saying that most questions are not very difficult to answer; often all it takes is just a yes or no, or naming the place/person/time etc. about which you have been asked.

This being said, we can group these question/answer pairs in three categories, which needsa certain type of answer.

Question type	Examples	Answer type	Examples
Questions <u>about an identified person or thing.</u> This includes all questions starting with "**do**", "**have**", or "**is**". In Italian they either start with the verb "**essere**" or "**avere**", or with a **noun/pronoun**.	Do you like pizza? Ti piace la pizza?	These questions open up for a **yes/no** type of answer.	No. I don't have a soul. No. Sono senz'anima.
	Is Mario home? Mario è a casa?		Yes, he is. Sì, è a casa.
	Did you take out the trash? Hai portato fuori la spazzatura?		No, I'm letting it ferment. No, la sto lasciando fermentare.
	Have you ever been in love? Sei mai stato/a innamorato/a?		Yes, with Jesus. Sì, di Gesù.
Questions <u>about an unidentified:</u> -<u>Place</u>, and usually start with: **Where (dove)** -<u>Person</u>, and usually start with: **Who (chi)**, Whose (di chi), with Whom (con chi) -<u>Thing or action</u>, and usually start with: **What (cosa, quale)**, Which (quale) -<u>Time</u>, and usually	Where are you from? Da dove vieni?	These questions can usually be answered by simply **naming the place/person/thing/etc.** at question.	I'm from the US. (Vengo)* dagli Stati Uniti. *or* Sono americano/a.
	Who are you? Chi sei tu? Whose wallet is this? Di chi è questo portafoglio?		I'm your worst nightmare. (Sono)* il tuo peggiore incubo It's mine now. È mio, da adesso.
	What did you do? Cos'hai fatto? Which one? Quale?		Nothing. He died on his own. Nulla. È morto da solo. This one.

123

start with: **When (quando)**, at what time (a che ora), how long (quanto) -<u>Amount</u>, and usually start with: **How much (quanto)**, How many (quanti) -<u>Modality</u>, and usually start with: **How (come)**			Questo/a.
	When are you going to leave? Quando partirai? How long does it take? Quanto ci vuole?		Tomorrow. Domani. About an hour. Circa un'ora.
	How much is a pizza margherita? Quanto costa una pizza margherita? How much pasta do you want? Quanta pasta vuoi?		Five euros. Cinque euro. I don't know. A normal serving. Boh**. Un piatto normale.
	How did you get here? Come sei/siete arrivato/a/i qui?		By bus. In pullman.
Questions which ask <u>about the reasonings</u> behind something, and usually start with: **Why (perché)**	Why did you not go? Perché non sei andato? Why do you want that toy? Perché vuoi quel giocattolo?	These questions are typically answered with a formulation that starts with **"because"** or "for". In Italian, they use **"perché"** for "because" as well as for "why". "For" is translated with "per".	Because I was sick. Perché stavo male. Because! Perché sì!

* the parts in brackets can be omitted.

** Boh is a very common Italian expression that is very badly explained in Spider-Man: Far from Home. What it means is just "I don't know, who knows", and it is used when you don't think you're supposed to know, or you don't care to know, or don't know how to know. Basically, when you're clueless or don't want to bother about finding the answer. It does not necessarily mean that you don't care or that you want to end the conversation, and it cannot translate either "I don't care" or "get out of my face". Don't listen to Zendaya/MJ.

Take-home message

Answering questions is pretty easy, as only 3 types of answers are usually required:

- yes or no;
- naming the person/thing/amount/time/etc. that is being asked to specify (who/what/how much/when/etc.);
- explaining why (perché) something is. [Remember that the Italian for "because..." is also "perché..."]

3.2
Making conversation

This chapter will be slightly different from what we've done so far. It will consist of just two tables, where a plausible conversation is reported. The conversations will contain several useful expressions, in the form of questions and answers, but don't worry: they're mostly expressions we already have encountered.

The first conversation will have a formal tone and will be in the polite form. The second conversation will be informal. The table will provide the translation and transliteration of the conversation in Italian. Easy-peasy, so let's get busy!

Conversation 1 - Polite form.

Scenario: An American man enters a B&B; the owner is an old Italian lady.

IT	EN	Transliteration
A: Buongiorno.	A: Hello.	*A: Boo-ohn-djohr-noh*
B: Buongiorno.	B: Hello.	*B: Boo-ohn-djohr-noh*
A: Vorrei sapere se avete una camera disponibile; non ho prenotato.	A: I would like to know if you have any available rooms; I didn't book (in advance).	*A: Vor-reh-ee saa-peh-reh seh aa-veh-teh oonaa kaa-meh-raa dis-pon-ee-bee-leh; non oh preh-no-taa-toh.*

B: Sì, abbiamo ancora due camere disponibili. Una per due persone con vista sulle colline e una per quattro persone con vista sul cortile interno.	B: Yes, we still have two available rooms. One for two people and a view on the hills, and one for four people and a view on the inner yard.	B: Sèè. ahb-bee-aa-moh ahn-koh-rah dooeh kaa-meh-reh dis-poh-nee-bee-lee. Oonaa per dooe per-soh-neh kon vees-tah sool-leh kol-lee-neh eh oonah per kwat-troh per-soh-neh kon vee-stah sool kor-tee-leh een-ter-noh.
A: Vorrei la prima stanza di cui ha parlato, se possibile.	A: I'd like (to have) the first room you spoke (told me) about, if possible.	A: Vor-reh-ee lah pree-mah staan-tzah dee kooee ah par-laa-toh, seh pos-see-bee-leh.
B: Certamente. Quanto pensa di restare?	B: Absolutely. How long do you think you are going to stay?	B: Tcher-taa-men-teh. Kwan-toh pen-sah dee rest-aa-reh?
A: Penso di restare fino a martedì mattina. Quanto costa il soggiorno a notte?	A: I think I'm staying until Tuesday morning. How much is the stay per night?	A: Pen-soh dee rest-aa-reh phee-noh ah mar-teh-dèè mat-tee-nah. Kwan-to kos-taa eel sodj-djor-noh ah not-teh?
B: Sono quaranta euro a notte, quindi centoventi euro in totale per tre notti.	B: It's 40 euros per night, so 120 euros in total, for three nights.	B: Soh-noh kwaa-raan-tah eh-oo-roh ah not-teh, kween-dee tchen.toh-ven-tee eh-oo-roh een tot-aa-leh per treh not-tee.
A: Perfetto, va benissimo.	A: Perfect, that sounds great.	A: Per-fet-toh, vah ben-ees-see-moh.
B: Ok, allora procediamo con la registrazione e poi le do la chiave della camera.	B: Ok, so let's proceed with the registration, and then I'll give you the key of the room.	B: Oh-keh-ee, al-loh-rah pro-tcheh-dee-aa-moh kon lah reh-djee-straa-tzee-oh-neh eh

		poh-ee leh doh lah kee-aa-veh del-lah kaa-meh-rah.
A: Ok, grazie.	A: Ok, thank you.	*A: Oh-keh-ee, graa-tzee-eh.*
B: Mi può dare un documento (d'identità)*?	B: Can I have your ID?	*B: Mee poo-oh daa-reh oon doc-oo-men-toh?*
A: Il passaporto va bene?	A: Is the passport ok?	*A: Eel pas-saa-port-oh vah beh-neh?*
B: Certo!	B: Sure!	*B: Tcher-toh!*
A: Ecco a lei.	A: Here it is. [the passport]	*A: Ehk-koh ah leh-ee.*
B: Molto bene, abbiamo finito. Le chiedo una caparra di cinquanta euro e poi le faccio vedere dov'è la sua stanza.	B: Very well, we have finished. I'm asking you for a 50 euro deposit, and then I'll show you to your room.	*B: Mol-toh beh-neh, ahb-bee-aa-moh phee-nee-toh. Leh kee-eh-foh oonaa kaa-par-rah dee tcheen-kwan-tah eh-oo-roh eh poh-ee leh fatch-tchoh veh-deh-reh dov-èh laa sooaa staan-tza.*
A: Ecco a lei.	A: Here you are. [while paying]	*A: Ehk-koh ah leh-ee.*
B: Grazie mille. B: Prego, mi segua.	B: Thank you very much. B: Please, follow me	*B: Graa-tzee-eh meel-leh.* *B: Preh-goh mee seh-gooah.*

* the parts in brackets are often omitted.

Conversation 2 - Informal

Scenario: An American man named Sam has a friend who introduces him to an Italian friend of his, named Marco. The conversation is between Sam and Marco.

IT	EN	Transliteration
A: Ciao, sono Marco, piacere!	A: Hi, I'm Marco, nice to meet you! (lit. (it's a) pleasure)	A: *Tchaaoh, soh-noh Maar-koh, pee-ah-tcheh-reh!*
B: Ciao, sono Sam, piacere mio!	B: Hi, I'm Sam, nice to meet you too! (lit. pleasure (is) mine)	B: *Tchaaoh, soh-noh Sam, pee-ah-tcheh-reh meeoh!*
A: Sei americano, giusto? Di dove?	A: You're American, right? Where (are you) from?	A: *Seh-ee aa-meh-ree-kaa-noh, djoos-toh? Dee Doh-veh?*
B: Sì, vengo da un paese vicino a Dallas, in Texas.	B: Yes, I come from a town near Dallas, in Texas.	B: *Sèè, ven-goh dah oon paa-eh-seh vee-tchee-noh a Daallaas, een Texaas.*
A: Ah, il Texas. Tutto è più grande in Texas, vero?	A: Oh, Texas. Everything's bigger in Texas, right?	A: *Ah, eel Texaas. Toot-toh èh pee-òò graan-deh een Texaas, veh-roh?*
B: Sì... tranne i cervelli, qualche volta.	B: Yeah... except for brains, sometimes.	B: *Sèè... traan-neh ee tcher-vel-lee, kwal-keh vol-tah.*
A: Hahaha. E come mai sei in Italia?	A: Hahaha. And why are you in Italy?	A: *Hahaha. Eh koh-meh maaee seh-ee een EE-tah-lee-ah?*
B: Per amore. Amore per i soldi. Sono qui per lavoro, ti sto prendendo	B: For love. Love for money. I'm here for work, I'm just kidding	B: *Per aa-moh-reh. AA-moh-reh per ee sol-dee. Soh-noh kwee per*

129

in giro.	you.	*laa-voh-roh, tee stoh pren-den-doh een djee-roh.*
A: Ho capito. È per questo che hai imparato l'italiano?	A: I see. Is this why you learned Italian?	*A: Oh ka-pee-toh. Èh per kwes-toh keh aaee eem-paa-raa-toh lee-taa-leeaa-noh?*
B: Sì, ma anche perché ho una nonna Italiana.	B: Yes, but also because I have an Italian grandmother.	*B: Sèè, mah aan-keh per-kéh oh oona non-naa EE-taa-lee-aa-nah.*
A: Sì? Di dove?	A: Is she? Where (is she) from?	*A: Sèè? Dee Doh-veh?*
B: Sicilia, vicino a Palermo.	B: Sicily, near Palermo.	*B: See-tchee-lee-ah, vee-tchee-no ah Paa-lehr-moh.*
A: Ho capito, ho capito. Dai*, che dici, ti va di giocare a biliardo?	A: I see, I see. Well, what do you say, would you like to play pool?	*A: Oh kaa-pee-toh, oh kaa-pee-toh. Daaee, keh dee-tchee, tee vah dee djoh-kaa-reh a bee-lee-ahr-doh?*
B: Si, dai*. Fammi prendere una birra prima però.	B: Yeah, why not. Let me grab a beer first, though.	*B: Sèè, daaee. Faam-mee pren-deh-reh oona beer-rah pree-mah per-òh.*

* "Dai" is an Italian filler word that, depending on context, translates a few different things (pretty different things). Most commonly, "Dai!" means "Come on!" or "Oh, come on!". When it's at the beginning of a sentence, though, it usually means "ok", "well", "let's see", or other expressions that suggest moving on with the conversation. On the contrary, when it's at the end of a sentence, it usually means "why not", "not so bad", "after all" or other expressions that basically say that the topic is no big deal.

3.3
Shopping and groceries

In this chapter, we are going to do the same thing we did in the last one and work with conversations to show the use of some expressions. However, since this is a themed lesson, we first have to look into some new vocabulary.

VOCABULARY

Shopping Vocabulary			
Bag	la borsa or il sacchetto	Purchase	l'acquisto
(credit) Card	carta (di credito)	Refund	il rimborso
Cart	il carrello	to Return	restituire
Cash	i contanti	Sales (discounts)	i saldi
Changing rooms	i camerini	Shopping	Shopping or Fare compere
Check-out/cashier's desk/till	il cassa	Shop assistant	il/la commesso/a
Discount	lo sconto	Size	la taglia

to shop for Groceries	fare la spesa	Small	la (taglia) Small
Large	la (taglia) Large	Tailor	Sarto/a
Medium	la (taglia) Medium	Tax-free	Tax-free

CONVERSATION 1 - POLITE FORM

Scenario: A customer is asking a shop assistant for some help.

IT	EN	Transliteration
A: Mi scusi, avrei bisogno delle scarpe.	A: Excuse me, I (would) need some shoes.	A: *Mee skoo-see, aav-reh-ee bee-son-'nyo del-leh skar-peh.*
B: Sì, mi dica, come posso aiutarla? (aiutare lei → aiutarla)	B: Yes, tell me, how can I help you?	B: *Sèè, mee dee-kah, koh-meh pos-soh aa-eeoo-taar-lah?*
A: Di questo modello avete il 44?	A: Of this model, do you have a (size) 10?	A: *Dee kwest-toh mod-el-loh aa-veh-teh eel kwaa-rahn-taa-kwaat-troh?*
B: Un attimo che controllo in magazzino. ... Sì, ce l'abbiamo. Ecco, tenga. Le provi.	B: (give me) a second to check (in) the warehouse. ... Yes, we have it (here). Here they are, here you go (lit. here, take). Try them on.	B: *Oon aat-tee-moh keh kon-trol-loh een maa-gaadz-dzee-noh.* ... *Sèè, tcheh laab-bee-aa-moh. Ehk-koh, ten-gah. Leh proh-vee.*
A: Mi sembra vadano bene.	A: It looks like (lit. "it seems to me that") they are ok (lit. they go well).	A: *Mee sem-brah vaa-daa-noh beh-neh.*

132

IT	EN	Transliteration
B: Ok, gliele lascio in cassa?	B: Ok, (do you want me to) bring (lit. leave) them at the check-out desk for you?	B: Oh-keh-ee, 'yeh-leh laa-shoh een kaas-sah?
A: Sì, grazie.	A: Yes, thank you.	A: Sèè, graa-tzee-eh.
B: Perfetto, arrivederci a presto.	B: Perfect, see you soon.	B: Per-feht-toh, aar-ree-veh-dehr-tchee ah pres-toh.

CONVERSATION 2 - POLITE FORM

Scenario: A customer is trying to purchase an item at the local market.

IT	EN	Transliteration
A: Mi scusi, quanto costa questo coltello?	A: Excuse me, how much does this knife cost?	A: Mee scoo-see, kwan-toh kos-tah kwest-oh kol-tel-loh?
B: Viene venti euro.	B: It goes (lit. comes) for 20 euro.	B: Vee-eh-neh ven-tee eh-oo-roh.
A: Mi sembra un po' troppo per un coltello così.	A: It sounds* a little too much for a knife like this.	A: Mee sem-brah oon poh trop-poh per oon kol-tel-loh ko-sèè.
B: Guardi, se vuole posso lasciarglielo a quindici euro.	B: Look, if you want I can make it 15€ for you (lit. I can leave it to you for 15€)	B: Gooaar-dee, seh voo-oh-leh pos-soh lah-sheeaar-'yeh-loh ah kween-dee-tchee eh-oo-roh.
A: Va bene, lo prendo.	A: Fine, I ('ll) take it.	A: Vah beh-neh, loh pren-doh.
B: Ok, le serve un sacchetto?	B: Ok, do you need a bag?	B: Oh-keh-ee, leh sehr-veh oon saak-ket-toh?

A: Sì, grazie.	A: Yes, thank you.	A: *Sèè, graa-tzee-eh.*
B: Ecco a lei. Buona giornata.	B: Here you are. (Have a) good day.	B: *Ehk-koh ah leh-ee. Boo-oh-nah djor-naa-tah.*

* In English, we use all five senses to describe things: it feels nice, it sounds great, it tastes good, etc. Italians basically only use one verb, the verb "to seem", "sembrare". There are a few exceptions, but it's something too specific to be investigated in this context.

3.4
Business and work

This chapter will be about work, and will be especially useful to those of you who might have a need, now or in the future, to do business in Italy or with Italian companies.

As usual, we'll take a quick look at some vocabulary, and then we'll get into the thick of the chapter.

Business Vocabulary			
Amount	la quantità	Fashion	la moda
Artisanal	Artigianale	Headquarters	il quartier generale
Bonus	il/i bonus (*boh-noos*)	Meeting	la riunione or il meeting
Boss	il/la capo/a	Office	l'ufficio
Business	l'attività (commerciale) or gli affari	Pay	la paga or lo stipendio
Contract	il contratto	Price	il prezzo
Deal	l'affare or l'accordo	Rate	la tariffa

Doing business	Fare affari	Secretary	la segretaria
Employee	l'impiegato/a or il/la dipendente	Taxes	le tasse
Employer	il datore di lavoro	Vacation days	i giorni di ferie

Once again, we're going to use a conversation to introduce some new expressions and, at the same time, get an idea of what a normal conversation flow sounds like; also, don't miss out on the chance to practice pronunciation.

CONVERSATION 1 - Informal

Scenario: Two colleagues talk about the tasks on which they are working.

IT	EN	Transliteration
A: Luca, scusa*, hai chiuso in contratto con il cliente americano?	A: Luca, hey, did you close the contract with the American client?	A: Loo-kah, scoo-sah, ahee keeoo-soh eel con-traat-toh kon eel klee-ehn-teh ah-meh-ree-kaa-noh?
B: Sì, dovremmo spedire l'ordine in giornata, perchè?	B: Yes, we're supposed to ship the order today, why (do you ask)?	B: Sèè, dov-rem-moh speh-dee-reh lor-dee-neh een djor-naa-tah, per-kéh?
A: Perché ho un altro cliente che mi ha chiamato oggi, ma non so se abbiamo ancora abbastanza articoli in magazzino.	A: Because I have another client who called me today, but I don't know if we still have enough items in the warehouse.	A: Per-kéh oh oon al-troh klee-ehn-teh keh mee ah keeaa-maa-toh odj-djee, maa non soh seh ahb-beeaa-moh ahn-kor-ah ab-bas-taan-tzah ar-tee-kol-ee een mah-ghadz-dzee-noh.

IT	EN	Transliteration
B: Sempre per le sedie? Quante ne vuole? Penso ne siano rimaste una trentina.	B: (Is it) still about the chairs? How many (of them) does he want? I think there are thirtyish left.	B: *Sem-preh per leh seh-dee-eh? Kwan-teh neh voo-oh-leh? Pen-soh neh see-aa-noh ree-mas-teh oonaa tren-tee-nah*
A: Ne vuole venticinque.	A: He wants 25 of them.	A: *Neh voo-oh-leh ven-tee-tcheen-kweh.*
B: Allora ci sono. Dobbiamo mandare la richiesta di rifornimento poi però	B: We have them, then. We'll have to send a restocking request then, though.	B: *Al-lor-ah tchee soh-noh. Dob-beeaa-moh maan-daa-reh lah ree-kee-ehs-tah dee ree-for-nee-men-toh poh-ee per-òh.*

* in this instance, "scusa" is used just to call for attention

CONVERSATION 2 - POLITE FORM*

Scenario: An employer is talking to his employee.

IT	EN	Transliteration
A: Scusa** Paolo, domani riusciresti ad arrivare mezz'ora prima?	A: Hey Paolo, could you get here a half-hour sooner tomorrow?	A: *Skoo-sah Pah-oh-loh, doh-maa-nee reeoo-shee-res-tee ahd ahr-ree-vaa-reh medz-dzoh-rah pree-mah?*
B: Penso di sì, ma per cosa, scusi?	B: I think I can, but what for, "if I can ask"?	B: *Pen-soh dee sèè, mah per koh-sah, scoo-see?*
A: Arriva un cliente australiano e vorrei che gli facessi fare un giro.	A: An Australian client is coming over, and I would like you to show him around.	A: *Ahr-ree-vah oon klee-ehn-teh aaoos-traa-leeaa-noh e vor-reh-ee keh 'yee faa-*

		tches-see faa-reh oon djee-roh.
B: Ah ok, non c'è problema.	B: Oh, ok, (there's) no problem.	*B: Ah oh-keh-ee, non tchèh pro-bleh-mah.*
A: Perfetto.	A: Perfect.	*A: Per-fet-toh*
B: Mi può dire il nome del cliente?	B: Can you tell me the name of the client?	*B: Mee poo-òh dee-reh eel noh-meh dehl klee-ehn-teh?*
A: Si chiama Paul Norman, mi pare.	A: His name's Paul Norman, I think (lit. "it seems to me").	*A: See keeaa-mah Paul Norman, mee paa-reh.*
B: Ok, grazie.	B: Ok, thank you.	*B: Oh-keh-ee, graa-tzee-eh.*

* The employer (A) is talking in a formal way, but he/she's not using the polite form. The employee (B) is using the polite form.

** in this instance, "scusa" is used just to call for attention

3.5
Dating and making friends

Now that we have covered the basics of making conversation, we can use our new knowledge and see how to make some small talk in Italian. In this chapter, we'll go over some common words and expressions that are used when talking to someone just to have conversation, or that have to do with dating and making friends. While most expressions are used in both contexts, some are understandably flirty.

As usual, let's start with the vocabulary.

Making-friends vocabulary			
Appetizer-dinner	Aperitivo*	Funny	Divertente or Simpatico/a**
Concert	Concerto	Hobby	Hobby (*ohb-bee*)
Club	Club or Discoteca	Job	Lavoro
Drink	Drink or Qualcosa da bere	Music	Musica
Eat	Mangiare	(phone) Number	Numero (di telefono)

Free-time	Tempo libero	Sport	Sport
Friend	Amico/a	Together	Assieme
Friendship	Amicizia	a Walk/Stroll	una Passeggiata

*Aperitivo is a social event, and a very important part of the Italian culture. It is essentially an early dinner (6 to 7.30 PM) with drinks. Italians typically have dinner between 7.30 and 9PM, so aperitivo is an early dinner to their standards.

**Simpatico can be translated with funny or nice, but it doesn't really have an English one-word translations, as it basically means "someone with whom you enjoy spending time".

Dating vocabulary			
Date	l'appuntamento	go to the Movies	Andare al cinema
Dinner out	la cena fuori	Heels (heeled shoes)	Scarpe col tacco
Dress	il vestito	Offer a drink	Offrire un drink or Offrire qualcosa da bere
to Flirt	Flirtare* (*flehr-taa-reh*)	to Pick up (car)	Passare a prendere
Flowers	i fiori	Perfume	Profumo
to Hold hands	Tenersi per mano	Romantic walk	Passeggiata romantica
Kiss	il bacio	Shirt	Camicia
to Kiss	Baciare	Suit (menswear)	il vestito or il completo

*this is our first example of foreign words that are transformed into Italian. They're often pronounced differently and might have a hybrid spelling.

This time, we won't look at whole conversations, but just some common questions and answers that can make up a real conversation.

IT	EN	Transliteration
Andiamo da un'altra parte? or Ti va se andiamo da un'altra parte?	Shall we go somewhere else? or Do you want to go somewhere else?	*An-deeaa-moh dah oon aal-trah par.teh?* *Tee vah seh...*
Che musica ti piace?	What music do you like?	*Keh moo-see-kaa tee peeaa-tcheh?*
Che hobby hai?	What are your hobbies?	*Keh ohb-bee aaee?*
Com'è il posto in cui abiti?	How is it where you live?	*Kohm'èh eel pohs-toh een kooee aa-bee-tee?*
Come stai? Tutto bene!	How are you? I'm ok! (it's kind of a standard answer)	*Kom-eh staaee?* *Toot-toh beh-neh!*
Cosa fai nella vita?**	What do you do for a living?	*Koh-sah phaa-ee nehl-laa vee-taa?*
Cosa ti va di fare?	What do you want to do? (lit. What do you feel like doing?)	*Kos-ah tee vah dee faa-reh?*
Dove abiti?	Where do you live?	*Dov-eh aa-bee-tee?*
Fai qualche sport?	Do you do any sport?	*Phaaee kwaal-keh sport?*

Quante lingue sai parlare?	How many languages can you speak?	*Kwaan-teh leen-gweh saaee paar-laa-reh?*
Ti passo a prendere alle (otto*).	I'll come and get you / pick you up at (eight).	*Tee pas-soh a prehn-deh-reh al-leh ot-toh.*

* We have seen so far that Italians normally use a 24-hour clock, but that's only true in a very formal environment or when there's a need to be precise. Most of the time, especially in speaking, Italians use a 12-hour clock, using "di mattina", "di pomeriggio", "di sera" and "di notte" for AM and PM, but only when it would be unclear without specifying.

** In Italian, you can ask about someone's occupation using expressions such as "che lavoro fai"? (lit. what job do you do?), but it's just as common to ask "what do you do in life?", like in this case.

3.6
Cooking

Our last lesson will be about cooking terminology. Food and cooking are a major part of the Italian culture, and it is not uncommon to hear Italians talk about cooking, even outside strictly related contexts. Many people just like to share recipes and ideas, and compare ingredients and cooking techniques.

As usual, we'll start off some vocabulary, and then we'll see a short conversation.

Cooking vocabulary			
to Boil	Bollire	to Fry	Friggere
to Broil	Arrostire	to Knead	Impastare
to Brown	Rosolare	Oven	Forno
Casserole	Casseruola	Pan	Padella
Chef	Chef	Pot	Pentola
to Cook	Cucinare	to Sauté	Saltare (in padella)
Cook	Cuoco/a	to Steam	Cuocere al vapore

Dish	Piatto	Stove	Fornello/i

Common ingredients			
Bread	Pane	Potatoes	Patate
Butter	Burro	Rice	Riso
Cheese	Formaggio	Salt	Sale
Egg	Uovo	Spices	Spezie
Flour	Farina	Sugar	Zucchero
Fruit	Frutta	Vegetables	Verdure
Milk	Latte	Vinegar	Aceto
Oil	Olio	Water	Acqua
Pepper	Pepe	Yeast/Baking powder	Lievito

Here is a possible conversations about cooking and food; A and B are peers having an informal chat, so neither of the two is using the polite form.

IT	EN	Transliteration
A: A te piace la pasta alla carbonara?	A: Do you like pasta alla carbonara?	A: Ah teh peeaa-tcheh laa paas-taa aal-laa kaar-boh-naa-raa?
B: Scherzi? La carbonara è il mio piatto preferito!	B: Are you kidding? Carbonara is my favorite dish!	B: Skehr-tzee? Laa kaar-boh-naa-raa èh eel mee-oh peeaat-toh preh-pheh-ree-toh!
A: Davvero?! Tu come	A: Really?! How do you	A: Daav-veh-roh?! Too

la fai?	make it?	*koh-meh laa phaaee?*
B: Per la salsa uso solo i tuorli delle uova, pepe, parmigiano e pecorino. Tu?	B: For the sauce I only use egg yolks, pepper, Parmesan and Pecorino cheese. (what about) You?	*B: Pehr laa saal-saa oo-soh soh-loh ee twohr-lee dehl-leh oo-oh-vaa, peh-peh. graa-naa eh peh-koh-ree-noh. Too?*
A: No, io uso anche un po' di albume.	A: No, I also use some egg whites.	*A: Noh, eeoh oosoh aan-keh oon poh dee aal-boo-meh.*
B: Ah, ho capito. E usi la pancetta o il guanciale?	B: Ah, I see. Do you use pancetta (pork belly) or guanciale (pork jowl)?	*B: Aa, oh kaa-pee-toh. Eh oosee laa paan-tcheht-taa oh eel gwaan-tchaa-leh?*
A: Il guanciale.	A: (I use) Guanciale.	*A: Eel gwaan-tchaa-leh.*
B: Anche io, è molto meglio.	B: Me too, it's way better.	*B: Aan-keh eeoh, èh mohl-toh me-'yoh.*
A: E tu la panna ce la metti?	A: And do you add cream? (lit. "to put in")	*A: Eh too laa paan-naa tcheh laa meht-tee?*
B: No, ci tengo alla salute.	B: No, I care about my health.	*B: Noh, tchee ten-goh al-laa saa-loo-teh*
A: Troppi grassi?	A: Too many fats?	*A: Trop-pee graas-see?*
B: No, è che sono di Roma. Se qualcuno a casa scopre che ho fatto la carbonara con la panna, mi ammazzano di botte.	B: No, the thing is that I'm from Rome. If someone at home finds out that I made carbonara with cream, they'll beat me to death.	*B: Noh, èh keh soh-noh dee Roh-maa. Seh kwaal-koo-noh aa kaa-saa sko-preh keh oh phaat-toh laa kaar-boh-naa-raa kon laa paan-naa, mee aam-maatz-tzaa-noh dee bot-teh.*

145

A: In effetti sarebbe il minimo che ti meriti.	A: That would be the least you deserve, indeed.	A: *Saa-rehb-beh eel mee-nee-noh keh tee meh-ree-tee.*

3.7
Let's practice!

This practice session will all be about finding the correct answer to a given question or vice versa. Are you ready? 20 multiple-choice exercises are coming up for you!

EXERCISES:

PART 1 - Answer the questions

1) Come ti chiami?

   A. A New York
   B. John
   C. Alle 21:00

2) Quanti anni hai?

   A. 35
   B. 1
   C. Blu

3) Da dove vieni?

   A. Vola
   B. Dagli Stati Uniti
   C. Per due adulti

4) Perché sei in Italia?

   A. Un caffè, grazie.
   B. Perché sono allergico alle noci.
   C. Per una vacanza.

5) Quanti biglietti vuole?

   A. 4, per favore.
   B. 21:00, se possibile.
   C. 13,50 €

6) Come la vuole la bistecca?

   A. Ho 15 anni
   B. Al sangue, grazie.
   C. Sono nato a New York.

7) Vuoi uscire a bere qualcosa stasera?

   A. Siamo a 43 km.
   B. Sono un designer.
   C. Sì, certo!

8) Quanti anni hanno i bambini?

   A. Sono 2.
   B. Hanno 8 e 11 anni.
   C. Sono 65 e 74 anni.

9) Buongiorno, come posso aiutarla?

   A. Buonasera, ti va di uscire con me?
   B. Salve, vorrei comprare queste scarpe.
   C. Ciao, sì grazie.

10) Devo saltare le cipolle?

   A. No, mangia due pentole.
   B. Sì, falle rosolare.
   C. Sì, due biglietti, grazie.

PART 2 - Find the most suitable question for the given answer

11) Alle otto di sera.

    A. Chi sei tu?
    B. Quanto costa questo?
    C. A che ora finisci di lavorare?

12) Ho 42 anni.

    A. Quante sono?
    B. Quanto costa?
    C. Quanti anni hai?

13) Sono americano.

    A. Che lavoro fai?
    B. Da dove vieni?
    C. Posso aiutarla?

14) Due biglietti per Roma per favore.

    A. Salve, come posso aiutarla?
    B. Buonasera, vuole del vino?
    C. Buongiorno, come stai?

15) No, grazie, sono allergico.

    A. Quanto costa visitare il Colosseo?
    B. Vorresti uscire a bere qualcosa con me stasera?
    C. Vuoi degli Smarties?

16) Dopo la hall sulla destra.

    A. Come ti chiami?
    B. Quanto ci vuole per arrivare a Roma?
    C. Mi scusi, dov'è il bagno?

17) Fino a martedì.

    A. Quanto tempo ci vuole per visitare il Colosseo?
    B. Fino a quando pensa di restare?
    C. Come hai fatto?

18) Mi piace il gelato.

    A. Qual è il tuo dessert preferito?
    B. Ti piace il cinema?
    C. Come si chiama tua moglie?

19) Sì, se possibile.

    A. Ha visto un labrador nero?
    B. Vuole la colazione domani?
    C. Quanto costa quel souvenir?

20)   Sta bene, grazie.

    A. Perché sta pagando?
    B. Dove sta la mia valigia?
    C. Come sta sua moglie?

ANSWERS	
1 → B	11 → C
2 → A	12 → C
3 → B	13 → B
4 → C	14 → A
5 → A	15 → C
6 → B	16 → C
7 → C	17 → B
8 → B	18 → A
9 → B	19 → B
10 → B	20 → C

PRACTICE

WITH EXERCISES

P.1
Pronunciation practice

You have completed all the lessons in this book, congratulations! It's now time for you to consolidate your new knowledge with some practice. While working on these exercises, try to enjoy your good results and not worry when you fall short; remember that our learning method is based on mistakes, and that sometimes we purposely have been having you face exercises that are probably too difficult for your level.

Without further ado, let's start practicing. The first two sessions are about pronunciation. Some exercises are based on simply saying or repeating a given expression, and because of that, although you can practice just by reading the transliteration, it would be especially useful to have the audiobook version of this book.

Pronunciation exercises - part 1

These exercises will target the pronunciation of single words, in the form of a multiple-choice question.

1) Find the correct transcription for the word "Biglietto". What does this word mean?

   A. By-gleht-toh
   B. Bee-glee-eht-toh

C. Bee-'yet-toh

2) Find the correct transcription for the word "Valigia". It means suitcase.

A. Vaa-lee-geeah
B. Vaa-lee-djee-ah
C. Vaa-lee-djah

3) Find the correct transcription for the word "Buongiorno". What does this word mean?

A. Bohn-djee-ohr-noh
B. Boo-ohn-djohr-noh
C. Boo-ohn-djee-ohr-noh

4) Find the correct transcription for the word "Chiesa". What does this word mean?

A. Kee-eh-sah
B. Tchee-eh-sa
C. Hee-eh-sa

5) Find the correct transcription for the word "Scoglio". It means sea rocks.

A. Shoh-gloh
B. Skoh-glee-oh
C. Skoh-'yoh

6) Find the correct transcription for the word "Foglio". What does this word mean?

A. Pho-'yoh
B. Fo-gh-lioh
C. Fog-lioh

7) Find the correct transcription for the word "Riunione". What does this word mean?

A. Reeoo-neeoh-neh

B. Roo-neeoh-neh

C. Reeoo-noh-neh

8) Find the correct spelling for the word that sounds like "baa-tchah-reh". What does this word mean?

A. Bacare

B. Baciare

C. Bachare

9) Find the correct spelling for the word that sounds like "toh-vaa-'yah". It means tablecloth.

A. Tovaglia

B. Tovagia

C. Tovaia

10) Find the correct spelling for the word that sounds like "gooee-dah". What does this word mean?

A. Guida

B. Giuda

C. Gueda

Pronunciation exercises - part 2

You're now asked to read and repeat some expressions, most of which we have already encountered throughout the book; help yourself with the transliterations and focus on the parts which you struggle the most with. If you want, you can record yourself with your phone, or other devices, and compare your pronunciation with the original one, to find your weak points.

1)

A: Ciao, come ti chiami?

B: Ciao, mi chiamo Luca. Tu come ti chiami?

A: Tchaaoh, koh-meh tee kee-ahm-ee?

B: *Tchaaoh, mee kee-ahm-oh Loo-kah. Too koh-meh tee kee-ahm-ee?*

2)

A: Mi scusi, mi può aiutare?
B: Sì, mi dica, come posso aiutarla?

A: *Mee scoo-see, mee poo-òh ah-ee-oo-tah-reh?*
B: *Sèè, mee dee-kah, koh-meh pos-soh ah-ee-oo-tahr-lah?*

3)

A: Buongiorno, vorrei sapere se avete una camera disponibile; non ho prenotato.
B: Sì, abbiamo ancora due camere disponibili. Quale vuole?

A: *Boo-ohn-djohr-noh, vor-reh-ee saa-peh-reh seh aa-veh-teh oonaa kaa-meh-raa dis-pon-ee-bee-leh; non oh preh-no-taa-toh.*
B: *Sèè. ahb-bee-aa-moh ahn-koh-rah dooeh kaa-meh-reh dis-poh-nee-bee-lee. Kwaa-leh voo-oh-leh?*

4)

A: Mi scusi, avrei bisogno delle scarpe. Di questo modello avete il 44?
B: Sì, salve, un attimo che controllo in magazzino.

A: *Mee skoo-see, aav-reh-ee bee-son-'nyo del-leh skar-peh. Dee kwest-toh mod-el-loh aa-veh-teh eel kwaa-rahn-taa-kwaat-troh?*
B: *Sèè, sal-veh, oon aat-tee-moh keh kon-trol-loh een maa-gaadz-dzee-noh.*

5)

A: Mi scusi, quanto costa questo coltello?
B: Costa dieci euro.

A: Mee scoo-see, kwan-toh kos-tah kwest-oh kol-tel-loh?
B: Kos-tah dee-eh-tchee eh-oo-roh.

6)

A: Quanti biglietti vuole?
B: Ne voglio 4, per 2 adulti e 2 bambini.

A: Kwan-tee bee-'yet-tee voo-oh-leh?
B: Ne vo-'yoh kwat-troh, per doo-eh aa-dool-tee eh doo-eh bahm-bee-nee.

7) *NEW*

A: Mi scusi, come si arriva al Colosseo?
B: Deve andare sempre dritto fino alla fine della strada, poi gira a destra e poi prende la prima a sinistra.

A: Mee scoo-see, koh-meh see ar-ree-vah ahl Koh-los-seh-oh?
B: Deh-veh an-daa-reh sem-preh dreet-toh phee-noh al-lah phee-neh del-lah straa-dah, poh-ee djee-rah ah des-trah eh poh-ee pren-deh lah pree-mah ah see-nees-trah.

A: Excuse me, how do I get to the Colosseum?
B: You have to go straight ahead until the end of the road, then turn right and then take the first on the left.

8)

A: Vuoi uscire a bere qualcosa una di queste sere?
B: Sì, perché no. Sei carino/a. *NEW*

A: Voo-oh-ee oo-shee-reh ah beh-reh kwal-koh-sah oonah dee kwest-eh seh-reh?
B: Sèè, per-kèh no. Seh-ee kaa-ree-noh/nah.

B: Yes, why not. You are cute. *NEW*

9)

A: Quanto pensa di restare in albergo?

B: Penso di restare fino a martedì mattina. Quanto costa il soggiorno a notte?
A: Sono quaranta euro a notte.

A: *Kwan-toh pen-sah dee rest-aa-reh een al-ber-goh?*
B: *Pen-soh dee rest-aa-reh phee-noh ah mar-teh-dèè mat-tee-nah. Kwan-to kos-taa eel sodj-djor-noh ah not-teh?*
A: *Soh-noh kwaa-raan-tah eh-oo-roh ah not-teh.*

10) *NEW*

A: Mi scusi, ha visto un bambino con una maglietta gialla?
B: No, mi spiace.

A: *Mee scoo-see, ah vees-toh oon bam-bee-noh kon oo-nah ma-'yeht-tah djaal-lah?*
B: *Noh, mee speeaa-tcheh.*

A: Excuse me, did you see a boy with a yellow t-shirt?
B: I have not, I'm sorry.

P.2
Tongue twisters

Tongue twisters are a simple and funny way to exercise on complex pronunciations. We will see 10 popular Italian tongue twisters, with sound transcription and translation (not that the meaning matters at all in this case). Try to repeat them a few times, speeding it up as you get more confident.

1)

Tigre contro tigre

Tee-greh kon-troh tee-greh

Tiger against tiger

2)

Trentatré trentini entrarono in Trento tutti e trentatré trotterellando.

Tren-taa-tréh tren-tee-nee en-traa-roh-noh een Tren-toh toot-tee e tren-taa-tréh trot-teh-rehl-laan-doh.

Thirty-three people from Trento entered Trento, all thirty-three jogging along.

3)

Ramarro marrone

Rah-maar-roh maar-roh-neh

Brown "European green lizard"

4)

Sopra la panca la capra campa, sotto la panca la capra crepa.

Sop-rah lah paan-kah la kaa-prah kaam-pah, sot-toh lah paan-kah lah kaa-prah kreh-pah.

Over the bench the goat lives, under the bench the goat dies.

5)

Li vuoi quei kiwi?

Lee voo-oh-ee kweh-ee kee-wee?

Do you want those kiwis?

6)

Dietro al palazzo c'è un povero cane pazzo, date un pezzo di pane a quel povero pazzo cane.

Dee-eh-troh ahl pal-aatz-tzo tchèh oon poh-veh-roh kaa-neh paat-tzoh, daa-teh oon petz-tzoh dee paa-neh ah kwehl poh-veh-roh patz-tzoh kaa-neh.

Behind a building there's a poor crazy dog, give a piece of bread to that poor crazy dog.

7)

Sereno è, sereno sarà e, se non sarà sereno, si rasserenerà.

Seh-reh-noh èh, seh-reh-noh saa-ràh eh, seh non saa-ràh seh-reh-noh see raas-seh-reh-neh-ràh.

Clear it is, clear it will be, and if clear it won't be, it will clear up. (the sky/weather)

8)

Sul tagliere gli agli taglia, che non tagli la tovaglia, la tovaglia non è aglio, se la tagli fai uno sbaglio..

Sool taa-'yeh-reh 'yee aa-'yee taa-'yah, keh non ta-'yee la toh-vaa-'yah, la toh-vaa-'yah non èh a-'yoh, seh lah taa-'yee phaaee oo-noh sbaa-'yoh.

On the chopping board garlic he/she cuts, cut he/she not the tablecloth, the tablecloth is not garlic, if you cut it you make a mistake.

9)

Ti ci stizzisci?? E stizziscitici pure!

Tee cee steetz-tzee-shee? Eh steetz-tzee-shee-tee poo-reh!

You get upset about that?? Go ahead and get upset about that!

10)

Forse Pietro potrà proteggerla.

For-seh Pee-eh-troh poh-tràh proh-tedj-djer-lah.

Maybe Pietro will be able to protect her.

P.3
Conversation exercises

This chapter and the next one will be about
conversation. In this chapter, we're going to practice
with multiple-choice exercises

FIND THE CORRECT ANSWER TO THE GIVEN QUESTION

1) Come ti chiami?

   A. Los Angeles
   B. Paolo
   C. Alle 20:00

2) Da dove vieni?

   A. Da New York
   B. Mi piace il blu
   C. No

3) Quanti anni hai?

   A. 312
   B. 29
   C. Grande

4) Vuoi uscire a bere qualcosa stasera?

   A. Ho perso le chiavi.
   B. Sono un fotografo.

C. Stasera non posso, ma sei carino, facciamo domani?

5) Buongiorno, come posso aiutarla?

    A. Avrei bisogno 4 biglietti per Roma, grazie.
    B. Con la bicicletta.
    C. Arrivo!

6) Quanti anni ha sua figlia?

    A. Ho 15 anni
    B. Ha 71 anni
    C. 15€

7) Stai partendo? Per dove?

    A. No, sono allergico.
    B. Sì, perché sono alto.
    C. Sì, per una vacanza.

8) Salve, avete una camera per 2 adulti e 2 bambini?

    A. No, sono tutte in mare.
    B. Sì, ne abbiamo 5 disponibili.
    C. No, non accettiamo animali.

9) Buongiorno, come posso aiutarla?

    A. Buonasera, ti va di uscire con me?
    B. Salve, vorrei comprare queste scarpe.
    C. Ciao, sì grazie.

10) Lei parla Italiano?

    A. No, sono estraneo al lessico e alla sintassi dell'italico idioma.
    B. Sì, ma solo un po'
    C. Sì, due biglietti, grazie.

FIND THE MOST SUITABLE QUESTION FOR THE GIVEN ANSWER

11) Dopo le 11.

    A. Chi è?

    B. Quanto costa?

    C. Da che ora sei libero?

12) Hanno 7 e 11 anni.

    A. Quante sono le mele?

    B. Quanto mangia una mucca?

    C. Quanti anni hanno le tue figlie?

13) Sono di Los Angeles.

    A. Che lavoro fai?

    B. Da che città vieni?

    C. Posso darti un bacio?

14) Due biglietti per Titanic, per favore.

    A. Salve, come posso arrivare a Roma?

    B. Buonasera, come posso aiutarla?

    C. Buongiorno, come sta la nave?

15) Sono allergico alle olive.

    A. Quanto costa il museo?

    B. Vorresti uscire a bere stasera?

    C. Hai preferenze sul cibo?

16) Dopo la chiesa, sulla destra.

    A. Quanti anni hai?

    B. Quanto ci vuole per arrivare a Napoli?

    C. Mi scusi, dove posso trovare una banca?

17) Domenica.

    A. Quanto è grande il suo bagaglio?

    B. Quando pensa di liberare la camera?

C. Come si fa il pesto?

18) Vorrei un gelato alla crema con la panna.

    A. Cosa le porto di dessert?
    B. Ti piacciono le barche?
    C. Quanti anni ha il cane?

19) Sì, se possibile.

    A. Ha visto un labrador nero?
    B. Vuole la colazione domani?
    C. Quanto costa quel souvenir?

20) Sì, eccola, grazie.

    A. Vuoi uscire con me?
    B. Dove sta il mio cappello?
    C. Se ha la carta studente, posso farle lo sconto studenti.

P.4
Conversation exercises - part 2

This second conversation practice will consist of 20 multiple-choice questions, of various kinds. More than one answer may be correct.

GENERIC QUESTIONS

1) How would you start a conversation with a shop assistant who's at the desk looking at you?

    A. Ciao ... can I see that candle-holder behind you?
    B. Buongiorno / Buonasera / Salve ... can I see that candle-holder behind you?
    C. Mi scusi ... can I see that candle-holder behind you?

2) How would you start a conversation with a shop assistant who's tidying up and is not looking at you?

    A. Mi scusi ... can you help me with some shoes?
    B. Buongiorno / Buonasera / Salve ... can you help me with some shoes?
    C. Ciao ... can you help me with some shoes?

3) What do you say in Italian when you pick up the phone?

    A. Ciao? Chi parla?
    B. Buongiorno? Chi parla?

C. Pronto? Chi parla?

4) You see a cute girl/guy sitting alone at the bar. How would you approach him/her?

   A. Buonasera, vuole venire a casa con me?
   B. Mi scusi, come posso aiutarla?
   C. Ciao, posso offrirti da bere?

5) How would you start a conversation with your professor?

   A. Buongiorno, professore, volevo chiederle ...
   B. Ciao, prof, volevo chiederti ...
   C. Salve, professore, volevo chiederle ...

TRANSLATE THE FOLLOWING QUESTIONS INTO ITALIAN

6) How old are you?

   A. Come sei vecchio?
   B. Quanti anni hai?
   C. Quanto sei vecchio?

7) How can I do that?

   A. Come posso fare quello?
   B. Come posso farlo?
   C. Come lo posso fare?

8) Why is it forbidden?

   A. Quando è vietato?
   B. Per chi è vietato?
   C. Perché è vietato?

9) Who is this girl?

   A. Chi è quella ragazza?
   B. Qual è quella ragazza?
   C. Chi sono quelle ragazze?

10) When are we leaving?

A. Quando partiamo?
B. Quando si parte?
C. Quando parte?

11) What do you mean?

A. In che senso?
B. Cosa intendi?
C. Cosa vuoi dire?

12) Where's the cathedral?

A. Dov'è la cattedrale?
B. Dove sta la cattedrale?
C. Dove si trova la cattedrale?

13) Which is mine?

A. Quale mio?
B. Quali sono i miei?
C. Qual è il mio?

TRANSLATE THE FOLLOWING STATEMENTS INTO ITALIAN

14) I'm sorry, I did not understand.

A. Mi spiace, non ho pagato.
B. Buonasera, non ho capito.
C. Mi scusi, non ho capito.

15) Can you repeat, please?

A. Può ripetere, per favore?
B. Puoi ripetere, per favore?
C. Poi ripeti, per favori?

16) Because I am blind.

A. Siccome sono cieco.
B. Per causa che sono cieco.
C. Perché sono cieco.

17) What's the number to call room service?

    A. Chi è il numero per chiamare il servizio in camera?
    B. Qual è il numero per chiamare il servizio in camera?
    C. Cosa è il numero per chiamare il servizio in camera?

18) Can I take my dog to the restaurant?

    A. Posso portare il cane al ristorante?
    B. Posso pagare il gatto al ristorante?
    C. Posso pagare il cane al ristorante?

19) Can you take a picture of us?

    A. Puoi farci una foto?
    B. Può farci una foto?
    C. Puoi prendere una foto di noi?

20)   Can I park here?

    A. Devo parcheggiare qui?
    B. Voglio parcheggiare qui?
    C. Posso parcheggiare qui?

P.5
Answers

<table>
<tr><td colspan="2" align="center">P.1 ANSWERS
Pronunciation exercises - Part 1</td></tr>
<tr><td>1 → C, ticket</td><td>6 → A, sheet (of paper)</td></tr>
<tr><td>2 → C</td><td>7 → A, meeting</td></tr>
<tr><td>3 → B, good morning or hello</td><td>8 → B, to kiss</td></tr>
<tr><td>4 → A, church</td><td>9 → A</td></tr>
<tr><td>5 → C</td><td>10 → A, guide or guidebook</td></tr>
</table>

<table>
<tr><td colspan="2" align="center">P.3 ANSWERS
Conversation exercises</td></tr>
<tr><td>1 → B</td><td>11 → C</td></tr>
<tr><td>2 → A</td><td>12 → C</td></tr>
<tr><td>3 → B</td><td>13 → B</td></tr>
<tr><td>4 → C</td><td>14 → B</td></tr>
<tr><td>5 → A</td><td>15 → C</td></tr>
<tr><td>6 → B</td><td>16 → C</td></tr>
<tr><td>7 → C</td><td>17 → B</td></tr>
<tr><td>8 → B</td><td>18 → A</td></tr>
</table>

9 → B	19 → B
10 → B	20 → C

P.3 ANSWERS Conversation exercises - part 2	
1 → B	11 → All three answers are correct
2 → A	12 → All three answers are correct
3 → C	13 → C
4 → C	14 → C
5 → A and C	15 → A and B
6 → B	16 → C
7 → All three answers are correct	17 → B
8 → C	18 → A
9 → A	19 → A and B
10 → A and B	20 → C

Conclusion

"If you talk to a man in a language he understands, that goes to his head. If you talk to him in his own language, that goes to his heart." - Nelson Mandela

1. Next steps to keep learning Italian

Congratulations on finishing the book! It's now time to put all that you have learned to good use. If you have been learning Italian because you're planning to travel to Italy, go and use your new knowledge. Otherwise, you can find Italians with whom you can practice, either in your town or online. There are several websites and apps that work like social networks for language exchange, and you can practice Italian with Italians while helping them with English.

If you enjoyed learning Italian, and are planning to pursue your studies, here is our recommendation on how to proceed.

At this point, you have reached a basic knowledge of the Italian language; you did that at a very high rate because of the learning method, but the downside to it is that you now have some incomplete knowledge, for example in relation to grammar and, for example, verb conjugations. That is probably your weakest point right now.

The best way to proceed, at this stage of learning, is diversifying the learning sources. We want you to divide and conquer. The macro-categories to be targeted are: grammar, vocabulary, pronunciation and practice.

LEARNING GRAMMAR

To improve your grammar, the best strategy is to work on good old books. You can try to get around it in different ways, but, at the end of the day, order and precision are what it takes to learn grammar at best. We will suggest some grammar books in the following subchapter.

Grammar is weird. It is the supporting backbone of a language, but it comes to life as a backward process, in retrospect. Languages are based on grammar, but languages are born before their grammars, as the rules are fixed once a language already exists.

Because of this unusual nature, grammar only partly makes sense. For those parts, books are your number one weapon. For the irregular, aberrant, crazy, and funny parts ... they might not be the best way. You can technically learn all the single pieces of information by heart and altogether, but that's just so depressing. Think of these as a second type of vocabulary, and take all your time to commit them to memory.

LEARNING VOCABULARY

To improve vocabulary, you can either watch Italian content, with subtitles in Italian (you can choose to watch a part of it in English, or with English subtitles, and then go back and change the language and subtitles to Italian and watch the same part again), or read books in Italian.

There are a lot of classic Italian books that were turned into simplified versions of themselves, specifically for learners; we'll name a few titles in the following subchapter.

LEARNING PRONUNCIATION

To improve pronunciation, you simply have to expose yourself to an Italian-speaking environment, and practice as much as you can. Movies and TV shows are great for this too, and alongside that you can practice with Italian speakers (for example in the ways mentioned above).

If you struggle with specific sounds, you might need a more speech-therapist-like way of learning. YouTube's guides are probably the best solution in this sense.

PRACTICING

Practice is always key to success. You can practice with people, sure, but you can also use practice-books, which are a great way to exercise, and you can do that while working on the rest of your learning.

There are all sorts of practice books: for grammar, for conversation, thematic, with workshops... the list goes on. Find the way that speaks the most to your soul and go for it. Remember that the only thing that is more important than practice is motivation, so do what you like and never forget to pursue it.

Most people have a reason to learn a language, or more than one. Whatever it is that fuels your engine, take advantage of it to keep on learning. Do you like Italian cuisine? Binge-watch cooking shows and YouTube tutorials. Do you like fashion? There's plenty of content about that too. The topic doesn't really matter, what matters is that it helps you learn, which makes it precious.

2. Recommended readings

If you enjoyed this book, the best way to tackle your grammar gaps is with our complementary workbook:

"Italian Workbook For Adult Beginners: Speak Italian in 30 Days!: Learn Italian Grammar & Vocabulary with Lessons, Activities, and Fun Exercises."

This book you just finished tried to promote your learning on the basis of a phrasebook, to set you up for going out there and living the language. This second book, its companion, is a workbook that is primarily focused on grammar and exercises, although it shares the same soul of this book and promotes learning through practice and mistakes.

If you're looking for something different, just know that you're breaking our heart doing that. We can't be friends anymore.

All jokes aside, classic grammar books are now so standardized that it is hard to express a strong preference towards a specific title, as they both bring the same results in the same way, pretty much.

Speaking of a different type of reading, in particular of the reading we mentioned to support learning vocabulary, we strongly recommend digging into the Italian classics. FOMO is a trending topic, but, for some reason, most people have very little fear of missing out on the classics of literature. Fools.

By exploring the learner's version of Italian classics, you'll have a chance to challenge yourself with the language while enjoying beautiful stories that have thrilled millions of people throughout dozens of generations.

Here are our favorite titles (each can be found in different difficulty levels):

- *La Divina Commedia*, released in 1320, by *Dante Alighieri*; a timeless classic that is basically an afterlife sci-fi in RPG.
- *I Promessi Sposi*, released in 1827, by *Alessandro Manzoni*; a beautiful love story in a book that is everything but a romance novel.
- *Il Decameron*, released in 1353, by *Giovanni Boccaccio*; a collection of incredible novels that take place in a plague-devastated Florence.
- *Il Principe*, released in 1532, by *Niccolò Machiavelli*; a political-strategy book created by one of the finest strategists that humanity has ever seen.

Alternatively, you can opt for something a little more recent, but consider that, the newer the book, the fewer learner's versions you can find. Here are the titles we like the most:

- *Se questo è un uomo*, released in 1947, by *Primo Levi*; the powerful story of a man who survived the Holocaust in the Auschwitz concentration camp.
- *Il fu Mattia Pascal*, released in 1906, by *Luigi Pirandello*; a novel about the troubled vicissitudes of a man who decides to change his life.
- *Uno, nessuno, centomila*, released in 1926, by *Luigi Pirandello*; the story of a wealthy man who falls into a crisis when his wife makes him notice that his nose is uneven.
- *L'amica geniale*, released in 2011, by *Elsa Ferrante*; the beautiful story of two girls of different social extraction growing up inNaples.
- *Gomorra*, released in 2006, by *Roberto Saviano*; an insightful novel about the real camorra, the mafia from Naples.

- *La coscenza di Zeno*, released in 1923, by *Italo Svevo*; a psychological novel that brings up the inner workings of an overthinker's mind.

These are all great artworks, just choose the topic that you fancy the most. The choice is only up to you.

This is the end of this chapter, and also of our journey together, at least for now. We might meet up again in a different book one day, but, for the moment, farewell, and remember: never stop learning!

QUICK

HANDBOOK

A. Making Conversation

BASIC EXPRESSIONS

Expressions for basic conversation		
EN	**IT**	**Transliteration**
Bye (formal) Bye (informal)	Arrivederci Ci vediamo or Ciao	*Ar-ree-veh-dehr-tchee* *Tchee veh-dee-ah-moh or Tchaaoh*
Excuse me (formal) Excuse me (informal)	Mi scusi Scusa or Scusami	*Mee scoo-see* *Scoo-sah or Scoo-sah-mee*
Good evening	Buonasera	*Boo-ohn-ah seh-rah*
Good morning	Buongiorno	*Boo-ohn-djohr-noh*
Hello (formal) Hello (informal)	Salve or Buongiorno Ciao	*Sahl-veh or Boo-ohn-djohr-noh* *Tchaaoh*
I'm sorry	Mi spiace	*Mee speeaa-tcheh*
No	No	*Noh*
Pardon me (formal) Pardon me (informal)	Mi scusi Scusa	*Mee scoo-see* *Scoo-sah*

Please	Per favore	*Pehr phaa-voh-reh*
Thank you	Grazie	*Graa-tzee-eh*
Yes	Sì	*See*
You're welcome	Prego	*Preh-goh*

EXPRESSIONS ABOUT MAKING CONVERSATION

Making conversation		
EN	**IT**	**Transliteration**
Absolutely!	Certamente! or Certo!	*Tcher-taa-men-teh! or Tcher-toh!*
Are you ...? (formal) Are you ...? (informal)	Lei è ...? Tu sei ...?	*Leh-ee èh ...?* *Too seh-ee ...?*
Can you **help** me?	Mi può aiutare?	*Mee poo-òh ah-ee-oo-tah-reh?*
Can you **hold the dog**?	Mi scusi, può tenere il cane?	*Mee scoo-see, poo-òh teh-neh-reh eel kah-neh?*
Can you take a **picture** of us?	Ci può fare una foto?	*Cee poo-òh fah-reh oo-nah pho-toh?*
Can you **tell me** ...?	Mi sa dire...?	*Mee sah dee-reh...?*
Do you mind if I ...?	Le spiace se ...?	*Leh spee-ah-tcheh seh ...?*
How old are you? I'm (n) years old.	Quanti anni hai? Ho (n) anni.	*Kwaan-tee ahn-nee ahee?* *Oh (n) aan-nee.*
I'm **looking for...**	Sto cercando...	*Stoh tcher-kahn-doh...*

Is there anyone who **speaks English**?	C'è qualcuno che parla inglese?	*Tch-èh kwahl-koo-noh keh par-lah een-gleh-seh?*
No, **I can't**.	No, non posso.	*Noh, non pos-soh.*
What's **your name**? My name is...	Come ti chiami? Mi chiamo...	*Koh-meh tee kee-aa-mee? Mee kee-aa-moh ...*
What do you do for a living?	Che lavoro fai?	*Keh laa-voh-roh phaaee?*
What **time** is it?	Che ore sono?	*Keh oh-reh soh-noh?*
Where's the **toilet**?	Dov'è il bagno?	*Dohv-èh eel bah-'nyoh?*
Yes, **I'd love to**.	Sì, volentieri.	*See, voh-len-tee-eh-ree.*
Yes, **I'd love to**.	Sì, mi piacerebbe molto.	*See, mee peeaa-tcheh-reb-beh mol-toh.*

B. Transportation and Renting

BASIC EXPRESSIONS

Expressions for basic conversation		
EN	**IT**	**Transliteration**
Bye (formal) Bye (informal)	Arrivederci Ci vediamo or Ciao	*Ar-ree-veh-dehr-tchee* *Tchee veh-dee-ah-moh or Tchaaoh*
Excuse me (formal) Excuse me (informal)	Mi scusi Scusa or Scusami	*Mee scoo-see* *Scoo-sah or Scoo-sah-mee*
Good evening	Buonasera	*Boo-ohn-ah seh-rah*
Good morning	Buongiorno	*Boo-ohn-djohr-noh*
Hello (formal) Hello (informal)	Salve or Buongiorno Ciao	*Sahl-veh or Boo-ohn-djohr-noh* *Tchaaoh*
I'm sorry	Mi spiace	*Mee speeaa-tcheh*
No	No	*Noh*
Pardon me (formal)	Mi scusi	*Mee scoo-see*

Pardon me (informal)	Scusa	*Scoo-sah*
Please	Per favore	*Pehr phaa-voh-reh*
Thank you	Grazie	*Graa-tzee-eh*
Yes	Sì	*See*
You're welcome	Prego	*Preh-goh*

VOCABULARY

Vocabulary you can find on tickets			
l'adulto	Adult	il numero	Number
gli anziani	Elderly	obliterare (or Validare)	To validate (the ticket)
l'arrivo	Arrival	l'ora (la ora)	Time (lit. hour)
i bambini fino ai … anni	Kids up to … years old	l'orario (lo orario)	Timetable or Designated (arrival/departure) time
il biglietto	Ticket	l'ordinario	Standard (fee, ride etc.)
il cambio (treno)	(Train) change	la partenza	Departure
l'extraurbano	Suburban	il/i passeggero/i	Passenger/s
il feriale (Fer.)	on Weekdays	il prezzo	Price
il festivo (Fest.)	on Holidays	i ragazzi	Young adults (usually people between 12 and 18 y.o.)
la fermata	Stop	lo scalo	Stopover

183

Vocabulary you can find on road signs			
l'aeroporto	Airport	l'imbarco	Boarding (the dock)
la casa circondariale	Prison*	l'ospedale	Hospital
i carabinieri	Carabinieri**	il parcheggio	Parking
il centro sportivo	Sports center	i pedoni (e.g.. pedoni a destra or zona pedonale)	Pedestrians (e.g. pedestrians on the right or pedestrian zone)
il centro (storico)	(Old) city center	il porto	Harbor
la chiesa	Church	le poste, sometimes "Poste Italiane" or "Poste e telegrafo"	Post office
il cimitero	Cemetery	la stazione	Train station
la farmacia	Pharmacy	il veterinario	Veterinary
il municipio	Town hall	la zona industriale	Industrial area

Transportation and renting vocabulary			
Bicycle	la bicicletta	(driver's) License	la patente (di guida)
Bike	la bicicletta/bici	Mobile home / trailer	la roulotte (roo-lot)
Boat	la barca	Motorbike	la moto
Boat	la barca/nave	Motorboat	il motoscafo
Bus	il bus/ l'autobus/	Motorcycle	la moto/

	il pullman *		motocicletta
Camper	il camper (kaam-pher)	Motorized scooter (stand-up scooter)	il monopattino elettrico
Car	l'auto(automobile)/macchina	Paddle boat	il pedalò
Car	l'auto/automobile / la macchina	Petrol	la benzina
Carriage (with horses) or car (on a train)	la carrozza	Plane	l'aereo/aeroplano
Climbing equipment	l'Attrezzatura da arrampicata	Pump (fuel)	il Distributore/ la Pompa di benzina
Contract	il Contratto	Quad bike/ATV	il Quad (kwohd)
Cost per day	il Costo al giorno	Scooter	lo Scooter/ il Motorino
Cost per hour	il Costo all'ora	Scooter or Vespa	lo Scooter or il Motorino
Distance	la Distanza	Ship	la Nave
Diving/snorkeling equipment	l'Attrezzatura da sub (soob)/da snorkeling (snor-keh-leeng)	Skis	gli Sci
Ferry (Boat)	il Traghetto	Subway	la Metro/ Metropolitana
(by/on) Foot	(a) Piedi	Sup	il Sup (Sup or Soop)
Gasoline	il Gasolio	Surfboard	la Tavola da surf (surf)
Helmet	il Casco	to Sign	Firmare
Inflatable boat	il Gommone	Train	il Treno
Insurance	l'Assicurazione	Tram	il Tram** (tr-raam)
Jacket	la Giacca	Trousers	i Pantaloni
Keys	le Chiavi	Yacht	lo Yacht (yot)

EXPRESSIONS ABOUT TRANSPORTATION AND RENTING

Transportation and renting		
EN	**IT**	**Transliteration**
A **ticket** to/for..., please.	Vorrei un biglietto per...	*Vohr-reh-ee oon bee-'yet-toh per...*
Are there **discounts** for... (students/kids/elderly)	Ci sono sconti per... (gli studenti/i bambini/gli anziani)?	*Tchee soh-noh skon-tee per... 'yee stoo-den-tee/ee bam-bee-nee/'yee ahn-tzeeah-nee?*
Can people with **disabilities** access your building/facility?	Le persone disabili riescono ad accedere al vostro edificio/servizio?	*Leh per-soh-neh dees-ah-bee-lee ree-es-koh-noh ahd atch-tche-deh-reh al vos-troh eh-dee-fee-tcho/ser-vee-tzee-oh?*
Can you **help** me?	Mi può aiutare?	*Mee poo-òh ah-ee-oo-tah-reh?*
Can you **tell me** ...?	Mi sa dire...?	*Mee sah dee-reh...?*
How much is a ticket to/for ...?	Quanto costa un biglietto per...?	*Kwan-toh kos-tah oon bee-'yet-toh per...?*
I'd like to **rent** (a car/a scooter/a pair of skis).	Vorrei noleggiare... (un'auto/uno scooter/degli sci).	*Vohr-reh-ee noh-ledj-djar-eh... oon-aoo-toh/oo-noh scoo-ter/deh-'yee shee*
I'm **looking for...**	Sto cercando...	*Stoh tcher-kahn-doh...*
Is there anyone who **speaks English**?	C'è qualcuno che parla inglese?	*Tch-èh kwahl-koo-noh keh par-lah een-gleh-seh?*

What time does (the train/plane/ferry) to (Rome) leave/pass?	A che ora parte/passa...(il treno/l'aereo/il traghetto)... per... (Roma)?	*Ah keh or-ah parteh/pass-sah...eel treh-no/lah-eh-reh-oh/eel trah-get-toh... per Roh-mah?*
Where do they sell **tickets** for (the bus/the subway/the ferry boat)?	Dove vendono i biglietti per (il bus/la metro/il traghetto)?	*Dov-eh ven-doh-noh ee bee-'yet-tee per eel boos/lah met-roh/eel trah-get-toh?*
Where does the (the train/plane/ferry) to (Rome) **leave from**?	Da dove parte...(il treno/l'aereo/il traghetto)... per... (Roma)?	*Dah doh-veh par-teh... eel treh-no/lah-eh-reh-oh/eel trah-get-toh... per Roh-mah?*
Where can I **find the timetable** for (the bus/the subway/the ferry boat)?	Dove posso trovare gli orari...(del bus/della metro/del traghetto)?	*Dov-eh pos-soh troh-vah-reh 'yee oh-rah-ree... del boos/del-lah met-roh/del trah-get-toh?*
Where's the **toilet**?	Dov'è il bagno?	*Dohv-èh eel bah-'nyoh?*
Where is ...?	Dov'è...?	*Dohv-èh...?*

C. Museums and Sightseeing

BASIC EXPRESSIONS

Expressions for basic conversation		
EN	**IT**	**Transliteration**
Bye (formal) Bye (informal)	Arrivederci Ci vediamo or Ciao	*Ar-ree-veh-dehr-tchee* *Tchee veh-dee-ah-moh or Tchaaoh*
Excuse me (formal) Excuse me (informal)	Mi scusi Scusa or Scusami	*Mee scoo-see* *Scoo-sah or Scoo-sah-mee*
Good evening	Buonasera	*Boo-ohn-ah seh-rah*
Good morning	Buongiorno	*Boo-ohn-djohr-noh*
Hello (formal) Hello (informal)	Salve or Buongiorno Ciao	*Sahl-veh or Boo-ohn-djohr-noh* *Tchaaoh*
I'm sorry	Mi spiace	*Mee speeaa-tcheh*
No	No	*Noh*
Pardon me (formal)	Mi scusi	*Mee scoo-see*

Pardon me (informal)	Scusa	*Scoo-sah*
Please	Per favore	*Pehr phaa-voh-reh*
Thank you	Grazie	*Graa-tzee-eh*
Yes	Sì	*See*
You're welcome	Prego	*Preh-goh*

VOCABULARY

MUSEUM AND SIGHTSEEING VOCABULARY			
Agritourism / Holiday Farm	l'agriturismo	Mountain hut	il rifugio
Audio guide/tour	l'audioguida	on Display	in mostra
Backpack	lo zaino	Opening time	l' orario di apertura
Beach	la spiaggia	Panoramic point / viewpoint	il punto panoramico
Beach lounger/chair	il lettino (da spiaggia)	Photos	le foto
Beach umbrella	l'ombrellone	Prohibition	il divieto
Bonfire	il falò or il fuoco da campo	Shop	il negozio
Cable Car	la funivia	Silence	il dilenzio
Camping	il campeggio	Ski resort	l'impianto sciistico
Closing time	l'orario di chiusura	Souvenir	il douvenir (soo-veh-neer)
Clothing rules	il codice/ le regole di abbigliamento	SPA / Thermal baths	la SPA / le terme
Exhibit	la mostra	Sunbathing	Prendere il sole
Fishing	la pesca or Pescare*	Sunscreen	la crema solare

189

Gallery	la galleria	Swim	Nuotare or Fare il bagno**
Group rate/discount	lo sconto comitiva	Swimsuit	il costume da bagno
Guide (book and person)	la guida	Tasting (food and wine)	la degustazione
Guided tour	la visita guidata OR il percorso guidato*	Track	il sentiero
Hike	l'escursione	Trekking guide	la guida ai sentieri
Horse ride	il giro/ la gita a cavallo	Trip	la gita
Lake	il lago	Winery	l'azienda vinicola

EXPRESSIONS ABOUT MUSEUMS AND SIGHTSEEING

Museums and sightseeing		
EN	**IT**	**Transliteration**
A **ticket** to/for…, please.	Vorrei un biglietto per…	*Vohr-reh-ee oon bee-'yet-toh per…*
Are you waiting (in **line**)?	Siete in coda	*See-eh-teh een koh-dah?*
Are there **discounts** for… (students/kids/elderly)	Ci sono sconti per… (gli studenti/i bambini/gli anziani)?	*Tchee soh-noh skon-tee per… 'yee stoo-den-tee/ee bam-bee-nee/'yee ahn-tzeeah-nee?*
Can I **enter the church** with these clothes?	Si può entrare in chiesa con questi vestiti?	*See poo-òh ent-rah-reh een kee-es-ah kon kwest-ee vest-ee-tee?*

Can I take **pictures** of the objects on display?	Si possono fare foto degli oggetti in mostra?	*See pos-soh-noh far-eh pho-toh de-'yee odj-djet-tee een mos-trah?*
Can I take pictures with **flash**?	Si possono fare foto col flash?	*See pos-soh-noh far-eh pho-toh kol flash?*
Can people with **disabilities** access your building/facility?	Le persone disabili riescono ad accedere al vostro edificio/servizio?	*Leh per-soh-neh dees-ah-bee-lee ree-es-koh-noh ahd atch-tche-deh-reh al vos-troh eh-dee-fee-tcho/ser-vee-tzee-oh?*
Can you **help** me?	Mi può aiutare?	*Mee poo-òh ah-ee-oo-tah-reh?*
Can you **hold the dog**?	Mi scusi, può tenere il cane?	*Mee scoo-see, poo-òh teh-neh-reh eel kah-neh?*
Can you take a **picture** of us?	Ci può fare una foto?	*Cee poo-òh fah-reh oo-nah pho-toh?*
Can you **tell me** ...?	Mi sa dire...?	*Mee sah dee-reh...?*
How long does the tour take?	Quanto dura la visita?	*Kwan-toh doo-rah lah vee-see-tah?*
How much is a ticket to/for ...?	Quanto costa un biglietto per...?	*Kwan-toh kos-tah oon bee-'yet-toh per...?*
I'm **looking for...**	Sto cercando...	*Stoh tcher-kahn-doh...*
I would like to rent a **beach umbrella** and two beach loungers.	Vorrei affittare un ombrellone e due lettini.	*Vor-reh-ee nol-edj-djar-eh oon om-brehl-loh-neh eh doo-eh let-tee-nee.*

191

Is it possible to have an **English guide** / audio guide / guidebook?	È possibile avere una guida/audioguida in inglese?	*Èh pos-see-bee-leh ah-veh-reh oonah gooee-dah/ah-oo-deeoh gooee-dah een een-gleh-seh?*
What **time** does the museum **open/close**?	A che ora apre/chiude il museo?	*Ah keh orah ap-reh/keeoo-deh eel moo-seh-oh?*
Where can I buy the **city pass**?	Dove posso comprare il city pass?	*Dov-eh pos-soh kom-prah-reh eel city paass?*
Where do they sell **tickets** for...?	Dove vendono i biglietti per...?	*Dov-eh ven-doh-noh ee bee-'yet-tee per...?*
Where's the **toilet**?	Dov'è il bagno?	*Dohv-èh eel bah-'nyoh?*
Where is ...?	Dov'è...?	*Dohv-èh...?*

D. Restaurants and Food

BASIC EXPRESSIONS

Expressions for basic conversation		
EN	**IT**	**Transliteration**
Bye (formal) Bye (informal)	Arrivederci Ci vediamo or Ciao	*Ar-ree-veh-dehr-tchee* *Tchee veh-dee-ah-moh or Tchaaoh*
Excuse me (formal) Excuse me (informal)	Mi scusi Scusa or Scusami	*Mee scoo-see* *Scoo-sah or Scoo-sah-mee*
Good evening	Buonasera	*Boo-ohn-ah seh-rah*
Good morning	Buongiorno	*Boo-ohn-djohr-noh*
Hello (formal) Hello (informal)	Salve or Buongiorno Ciao	*Sahl-veh or Boo-ohn-djohr-noh* *Tchaaoh*
I'm sorry	Mi spiace	*Mee speeaa-tcheh*
No	No	*Noh*
Pardon me (formal)	Mi scusi	*Mee scoo-see*

Pardon me (informal)	Scusa	*Scoo-sah*
Please	Per favore	*Pehr phaa-voh-reh*
Thank you	Grazie	*Graa-tzee-eh*
Yes	Sì	*See*
You're welcome	Prego	*Preh-goh*

VOCABULARY

Restaurant and food vocabulary			
Bar (pub, club)	il bar (il pub, la discoteca)	Plate	il piatto
Barman	il barman/ il barista	Receipt	lo scontrino
to Book	Prenotare	Restaurant	il ristorante
Beers	la birra in bottiglia Birra piccola (10 oz) Birra media (14 oz) Pinta di birra (17 oz) Birra da litro (34 oz)	Salt	il sale
Bill	il conto	Shaken, not stirred	Agitato, non mescolato
Chopsticks	le bacchette (cinesi)	Split the bill	Dividere il conto
Drink	il drink	Spoon	il cucchiaio

Fork	la forchetta	Stake (blue, red, medium red, medium, medium well, well done)	la bistecca or la costata: blue, al sangue, media / al sangue, media cottura, media / ben cotta, ben cotta
Leftovers	gli avanzi	Table	il Tavolo
Knife	il coltello	Take-out	l'asporto, or il Take-away, or la consegna a domicilio
Gelateria	la gelateria	Tip	la mancia
Glass (a glass)	il bicchiere	Toilet	La toilette (*twah-let*), or il bagno, or i servizi
Pizzeria	la pizzeria	Waiter/weitress	il cameriere/ la cameriera
Parmesan	il parmigiano / il formaggio grattugiato	Water (tap, bottled, uncarbonated, carbonated)	l'acqua: del rubinetto, in bottiglia, naturale, gassata o frizzante
Pepper	il pepe	Wine (red, white, pink)	il vino: rosso, rosa, rosé

EXPRESSIONS ABOUT RESTAURANTS AND FOOD

Restaurants and food		
EN	**IT**	**Transliteration**
A **table** for... (2), please.	Vorrei un tavolo per...(due), per favore.	*Vohr-reh-ee oon tah-voh-loh per... (doo-eh), per phaa-voh-reh.*
Can people with **disabilities** access your building/facility?	Le persone disabili riescono ad accedere al vostro edificio/servizio?	*Leh per-soh-neh dees-ah-bee-lee ree-es-koh-noh ahd atch-tche-deh-reh al vos-troh eh-dee-fee-tcho/ser-vee-tzee-oh?*
*May*you **help** me?	Mi può aiutare?	*Mee poo-òh ah-ee-oo-tah-reh?*
Can you **tell me** ...?	Mi sa dire...?	*Mee sah dee-reh...?*
I'm **allergic**/intolerant to... (gluten, strawberries).	Sono allergico/intollerante... (al glutine, alle fragole)	*Soh-noh al-ler-djee-koh/een-tol-leh-rahn-teh...al gloo-tee-neh, al-leh fra-go-leh*
I would like to **book a table** for four people at 9 PM.	Vorrei prenotare un tavolo per quattro persone per le 21.	*Vor-reh-ee preh-no-tah-reh oon tah-voh-loh per kwat-troh per-soh-neh per leh vent-oo-noh*
I would like to order a pizza with **delivery**.	Vorrei ordinare una pizza con consegna a domicilio.	*Vor-reh-ee or-dee-nah-reh oonah pitz-tza kon kon-seh-'nee-ah ah doh-mee-tchee-lee-oh.*
Is it possible to take **leftovers home**?	È possibile portare a casa gli avanzi?	*Èh pos-see-bee-leh por-tah-reh ah cah-sah 'yee ah-vaan-tzee?*

| Is there anyone who **speaks English**? | C'è qualcuno che parla inglese? | Tch-èh kwa, keh par-lah seh? |
| Where's the **toilet**? | Dov'è il bagno? | Dohv-èh eel ba, |

E. Shopping and Groceries

BASIC EXPRESSIONS

Expressions for basic conversation		
EN	**IT**	**Transliteration**
Bye (formal)	Arrivederci	*Ar-ree-veh-dehr-tchee*
Bye (informal)	Ci vediamo or Ciao	*Tchee veh-dee-ah-moh or Tchaaoh*
Excuse me (formal)	Mi scusi	*Mee scoo-see*
Excuse me (informal)	Scusa or Scusami	*Scoo-sah or Scoo-sah-mee*
Good evening	Buonasera	*Boo-ohn-ah seh-rah*
Good morning	Buongiorno	*Boo-ohn-djohr-noh*
Hello (formal)	Salve or Buongiorno	*Sahl-veh or Boo-ohn-djohr-noh*
Hello (informal)	Ciao	*Tchaaoh*
I'm sorry	Mi spiace	*Mee speeaa-tcheh*
No	No	*Noh*
Pardon me (formal)	Mi scusi	*Mee scoo-see*

Pardon me (informal)	Scusa	*Scoo-sah*
Please	Per favore	*Pehr phaa-voh-reh*
Thank you	Grazie	*Graa-tzee-eh*
Yes	Sì	*See*
You're welcome	Prego	*Preh-goh*

VOCABULARY

Shopping vocabulary			
Bag	la borsa or il sacchetto	Purchase	l'acquisto
(credit) Card	Carta (di credito)	Refund	il rimborso
Cart	il carrello	to Return	Restituire
Cash	i contanti	Sales (discounts)	i saldi
Changing rooms	i camerini	Shopping	Shopping or Fare compere
Check-out/cashier's desk/till	il cassa	Shop assistant	il/la commesso/a
Discount	lo sconto	Size	la taglia
to shop for Groceries	fare la spesa	Small	la (taglia) Small
Large	la (taglia) Large	Tailor	Sarto/a
Medium	la (taglia) Medium	Tax-free	Tax-free

EXPRESSIONS ABOUT SHOPPING AND GROCERIES

Shopping and groceries		
EN	**IT**	**Transliteration**
Are you waiting (in **line**)?	Siete in coda?	*See-eh-teh een koh-dah?*
Can people with **disabilities** access your building/facility?	Le persone disabili riescono ad accedere al vostro edificio/servizio?	*Leh per-soh-neh dees-ah-bee-lee ree-es-koh-noh ahd atch-tche-deh-reh al vos-troh eh-dee-fee-tcho/ser-vee-tzee-oh?*
Can you **help** me?	Mi può aiutare?	*Mee poo-òh ah-ee-oo-tah-reh?*
Can you **tell me** ...?	Mi sa dire...?	*Mee sah dee-reh...?*
How much is it?	Quanto costa?	*Kwan-toh kos-tah?*
I'm **looking for...**	Sto cercando...	*Stoh tcher-kahn-doh...*
Is there anyone who **speaks English**?	C'è qualcuno che parla inglese?	*Tch-èh kwahl-koo-noh keh par-lah een-gleh-seh?*
Where's the **toilet**?	Dov'è il bagno?	*Dohv-èh eel bah-'nyoh?*
Where is ...?	Dov'è...?	*Dohv-èh...?*

F. Emergencies

BASIC EXPRESSIONS

Expressions for basic conversation		
EN	**IT**	**Transliteration**
Bye (formal)	Arrivederci	*Ar-ree-veh-dehr-tchee*
Bye (informal)	Ci vediamo or Ciao	*Tchee veh-dee-ah-moh or Tchaaoh*
Excuse me (formal)	Mi scusi	*Mee scoo-see*
Excuse me (informal)	Scusa or Scusami	*Scoo-sah or Scoo-sah-mee*
I'm sorry	Mi spiace	*Mee speeaa-tcheh*
No	No	*Noh*
Please	Per favore	*Pehr phaa-voh-reh*
Thank you	Grazie	*Graa-tzee-eh*
Yes	Sì	*See*
You're welcome	Prego	*Preh-goh*

VOCABULARY

Emergency Vocabulary			
911	il 112	Injured	Ferito
Accident	l'incidente	Officer	l'agente
Ambulance	l'ambulanza	Police	la polizia
Bomb	la bomba	Red cross	la croce rossa
Broken	Rotto	Rescue team	la squadra di soccorso
Doctor	il dottore or il medico	Severe	Grave
Drunk	Ubriaco	Shoots	gli spari
ER	PS (Pronto Soccorso)	SOS	l' SOS (sohs or es-seh oh es-seh)
Fire	l'incendio	Stolen	Rubato
Fireman	Vigile del Fuoco	Surgery	l'operazione chirurgica
Help!	Aiuto!	to Arrest	Arrestare
Hospital	l'ospedale	to feel it Hurt	Fare male

EXPRESSIONS ABOUT EMERGENCIES

Emergencies		
EN	**IT**	**Transliteration**
Excuse me, can you **help me**? [informal] Excuse me, can you help me? [polite]	Scusa, mi puoi aiutare? Mi scusi, mi può aiutare?	*Scoo-sah, mee poo-òh ah-eeoo-tah-reh?* *Mee scoo-see, mee poo-òh ah-eeoo-tah-reh?*
How's (my husband)?	Come sta (mio marito)?	*Kom-eh stàh (meeoh maa-ree-toh?)*
I **can't find** my daughter, can you help me?	Non trovo più mia figlia, mi può aiutare?	*Non troh-voh pee-òò meeah phee-'yah, mee poo-òh aa-eeoo-taa-reh?*

I **feel a pain** in my chest.	Sento un dolore al petto.	*Sen-toh oon doh-loh-reh nehl pet-toh.*
I feel like **fainting**.	Mi sento svenire.	*Mee sen-toh sveh-nee-reh.*
I have an issue with my **car**.	Ho un problema alla macchina.	*Oh oon proh-bleh-mah al-lah maak-kee-nah*
I have **nausea**. I feel like vomiting.	Ho la nausea. Mi viene da vomitare.	*Oh lah now-seh-ah. Mee vee-eh-neh daa voh-mee-taa-reh.*
I heard **gunshots**!	Ho sentito degli spari!	*Oh sen-tee-toh de-'yee spa-ree!*
I lost my wallet / phone.	Ho perso il portafogli / il cellulare.	*Oh per-soh eel por-tah-pho-'yee / eel tchel-loo-lah-reh.*
I need an **ambulance**.	Ho bisogno di un'ambulanza.	*Oh bee-so-'nyo dee oon am-boo-lahn-tzah*
I think I have a **broken leg**.	Credo di avere una gamba rotta.	*Kreh-doh dee aa-veh-reh oo-nah gaam-bah rot-tah.*
I'm **looking for**...	Sto cercando...	*Stoh tcher-kahn-doh...*
Is it **bad**? Should I be **worried d**?	È grave? Mi dovrei preoccupare?	*Èh graa.veh? Mee dov-reh-ee preh-ok-koo-paa-reh?*
Is there a **toilet**?	C'è un bagno?	*Tchèh oon bah-'nyoh?*
Is there anyone who **speaks English**?	C'è qualcuno che parla inglese?	*Tch-èh kwahl-koo-noh keh par-lah een-gleh-seh?*
My arm **hurts**.	Mi fa male il braccio.	*Mee pha maa-leh eel braatch-tcho.*
Sorry, can you **give me a hand**? [informal]	Scusa, mi puoi dare una mano?	*Scoo-sah mee poo-oh-ee daa-reh oo-nah maa-noh?*
There's a woman who felt sick, **call 911**.	C'è una donna che si è sentita male, chiamate il **112**.	*Tchè oon-ah don-nah keh see èh sen-tee-tah maa-leh, keeaa-maa-teh*

		eel tchen-toh-doh-dee-tchee.
There's a **bomb alert** in the subway.	C'è un allarme bomba nella metro.	*Tchè oon al-lar-meh bom-bah nel-lah met-roh.*
They **kidnapped** my son!	Hanno rapito mio figlio!	*An-noh raa-pee-toh meeoh phee-'yoh!*
They **stole** my bag / my phone.	Mi hanno rubato la borsa / il cellulare.	*Mee an-noh roo-baa-toh lah bor-sah / eel tchel-loo-laa-reh.*
Where is ...?	Dov'è...?	*Dohv-èh...?*
Where's the **ER**?	Dove si trova il Pronto Soccorso?	*Doh-veh see troh-vah eel pron-toh sok-kor-soh?*

Made in the USA
Las Vegas, NV
25 November 2024

12579767R00125